George III

Very Interesting People

VIP

Bite-sized biographies of Britain's most fascinating historical figures

George III

Very Interesting People

John Cannon

OXFORD
UNIVERSITY PRESS

OXFORD
UNIVERSITY PRESS

Great Clarendon Street, Oxford ox2 6DP

Oxford University Press is a department of the University of Oxford.
It furthers the University's objective of excellence in research, scholarship,
and education by publishing worldwide in

Oxford New York

Auckland Cape Town Dar es Salaam Hong Kong Karachi
Kuala Lumpur Madrid Melbourne Mexico City Nairobi
New Delhi Shanghai Taipei Toronto

With offices in

Argentina Austria Brazil Chile Czech Republic France Greece
Guatemala Hungary Italy Japan Poland Portugal Singapore
South Korea Switzerland Thailand Turkey Ukraine Vietnam

Oxford is a registered trade mark of Oxford University Press
in the UK and in certain other countries

Published in the United States
by Oxford University Press Inc., New York

First published in the *Oxford Dictionary of National Biography* 2004
This paperback edition first published 2007

© Oxford University Press 2007

Database right Oxford University Press (maker)

First published 2007

British Library Cataloguing in Publication Data

Data available

Library of Congress Cataloging in Publication Data

Data available

Typeset by SPI Publisher Services, Pondicherry, India
Printed in Great Britain
on acid-free paper by
Ashford Colour Press Ltd., Gosport, Hants.

ISBN 978–0–19–921357–3 (Pbk.)

10 9 8 7 6 5 4 3 2 1

Contents

Preface

'The reputation of King George III has bene-fited from two apotheoses, one in his own life-time, the other two hundred years later. During the first decades of his reign the young king came in for heavy criticism. His devotion to his tutor, Lord Bute, brought down the wrath of those Englishmen, no small number, who dis-liked the Scots. His detestation of John Wilkes and his determination not to yield to popular pressure made the king more enemies. By 1771 the sinister *Junius* could remark 'nature intended him only for a good-humoured fool...a systemat-ical education has made him, by long practice, a consummate hypocrite'. The war with the Amer-ican colonists brought George III fresh antago-nists. Tom Paine dismissed him in *Common Sense* (1776) as 'the royal brute', and the Declaration of Independence the same year, in more stately language, denounced him as 'a tyrant, unfit to rule a free people'. In 1783 the king contemplated abdication. But transformation was swift. The extravagancies of his son, George, prince of Wales, made the king seem, by comparison, homely and sensible: his frugality contrasted with the prince's indifference to spending other people's money, and his irreproachable domestic life with the raffishness of the prince and his friends. The king's protracted illness in 1788–9 brought him much pity and sympathy. It needed only the atrocities of the French Revolution to transform him into a rock of stability in a monstrous and lunatic world.

The nineteenth century saw his reputation sink once more, as numerous memoirs and letters, many of them from his whig opponents, found their way into print. Horace Walpole's *Memoirs of George III* (1845), followed by *The Bedford Correspondence*, edited by the apostolic whig Lord John Russell (1842–6) and the *Memoirs of Lord Rockingham* (1852), depicted him as a would-be absolutist. Though J. W. Croker, for one, protested at this poisoning of the wells of history, historians took them at their face value and vied with each other in the exhuberance of their denunciations. G. O. Trevelyan stated that 'George III invariably declared himself on the wrong side in a controversy' (1880). W. E. H. Lecky was in total agreement (1882): 'it may be said, without exaggeration, that George III inflicted more profound and enduring injuries upon his country than any other modern king'. What Lecky would have said with exaggeration beggars belief. J. B. Bury, apostle of 'scientific' history, insisted that 'the American war was determined by the personal character of George III' (1902).

Once more the relief force was at hand. Romney Sedgwick's edition of the letters of the king to Bute (1939) demonstrated that they had no absolutist intentions. In 1953 Lewis Namier declared that he had never found the king a dissembler or a schemer. John Brooke, Namier's disciple, in a brilliant biography (1972) demonstrated the king's good taste and interest in books, music, astronomy, and science. George also benefited from a more compassionate attitude to mental alienation. A sumptuous exhibition at the Queen's gallery, Buckingham Palace, in 2004 provided yet more evidence of his wide interests. It has taken a long time to do justice to a man who found life difficult and whose suffering was appalling.

John Cannon

August 2006

About the author

John Cannon is Emeritus Professor of Modern History at the University of Newcastle upon Tyne. His books include *Parliamentary Reform, 1660–1832* (1973), *Aristocratic Century* (1984), and *Samuel Johnson and the Politics of Hanoverian England* (1994); he is also editor of *The Oxford Companion to British History* (1997).

'Born and educated in this country'

George III (1738–1820),

king of the United Kingdom of Great Britain and Ireland, and king of Hanover, was the second child and eldest son of Frederick Lewis, prince of Wales (1707–1751), and his wife, Augusta (1719–1772) of Saxe-Gotha. He was the first prince of Wales to be born in England since Charles II in 1630, which he turned to advantage in his accession speech of 1760: 'Born and educated in this country, I glory in the name of Britain' (Brooke, *King George the Third*, 390).

Both his parents had been educated in Germany and spoke German as their native tongue. Since his father had been forbidden St James's Palace in 1737, after the quarrel over the birth of his first child, Princess Augusta, George was born in the duke of Norfolk's house in St James's Square, on 24 May 1738. He was privately baptized by the bishop of Oxford at 11 p.m. on the day of his birth as there were doubts whether he would live; he was publicly baptized George William Frederick at Norfolk House on 21 June. At the age of ten he appeared in a family performance of Addison's *Cato*, and spoke a new prologue: 'What, tho' a boy! It may with truth be said, A boy in *England* born, in England bred' (*Gentleman's Magazine*, 19, 1749, 37).

A prince's childhood

Estimates of George's ability have varied. Horace Walpole was responsible for the story that he could not read English at the age of eleven, but Walpole cherished a deep dislike of the prince and his mother (Walpole, *Memoirs*, 1.56). George's father complained that he did not sufficiently care to please—no unusual remark for a father—and in a long conversation in 1752 with George Bubb Dodington the princess confessed that 'she wished that he was a little more forward, and less childish, at his age', and that all his affection was focused on his younger brother Edward (*Diary of … Dodington*, 151). The historian Romney Sedgwick thought that there were signs of mental retardation, but John Brooke produced evidence that the prince could read and write English and German by the age of eight, and that from the age of eleven he received systematic schooling from George Lewis Scott. The truth seems to be that he was a boy of average ability, rather reserved, and surrounded by tutors like Lord Harcourt and Thomas Hayter, bishop of Norwich, who were not particularly stimulating. In another conversation with Dodington in 1755 the princess admitted that her son was 'shy and backward ... but, with those he was acquainted, applicable and intelligent' (ibid., 317). But in later life he spoke French and German, was keenly interested in astronomy and clocks, drew and painted well, was fond of chess, and was a great collector of books. He was devoted to music, played the flute and harpsichord, and confided to Fanny Burney that he found it as strange to meet people who had no ear for music as to meet people who were dumb. The most detailed analysis of his character was made by Lord Waldegrave, who took over as governor from Harcourt, obliged to resign in 1752 after complaining that George was being brought up on Jacobite, in other words autocratic, notions. 'His parts', wrote

Waldegrave, 'tho' not excellent, will be found very tolerable'. He was 'uncommonly indolent' and had 'a kind of unhappiness in his temper' which led him to become 'sullen and silent', and to retire to his room 'to indulge the melancholy enjoyment of his own ill humor' (*Memoirs and Speeches*, 148–9). Some of these characteristics disappeared as he grew older. Indolence was replaced by restless activity, and inattention by meticulousness—his letters and memos dated to the precise minute. But an attribute which did remain was a tendency to censoriousness—'his religion', wrote Waldegrave, 'is not of the most charitable sort: he has rather too much attention to the sins of his neighbour' (ibid.)—and he frequently complained that it was his misfortune to live in peculiarly wicked times (ibid., 176–7).

The death of his father when George was twelve was unfortunate, less because Frederick might have been a good influence on him than because it meant that the burdens of state would fall on him early in life. Frederick left a political testament for his son, drafted in 1749. He was advised to separate Hanover from England, as George I had suggested, practise economy, and reduce the national debt. It concluded by advising George to 'convince the nation that you are not only an Englishman born and bred, but that you are also this by inclination' (G. Young, *Poor Fred: the People's Prince*, 1937, 174). There was no suggestion that royal authority must be strengthened or that political parties should be eradicated. But the extirpation of parties was something of a commonplace at the time. Viscount Bolingbroke had denounced them in a *Dissertation upon Parties* (1733–4) and in *The Idea of a Patriot King* (1749), and Frederick had promised to eradicate them in his contract with the tories in 1747.

The rise of Bute

Waldegrave's welcome at Leicester House in 1752 wore thin, and by 1756 he was glad to give way. His influence had already been replaced by that of John Stuart, third earl of Bute. Bute had been a lord of the bedchamber to Prince Frederick in 1750, but he was retained by the princess after her husband's death to help plan Kew Gardens. Prince George was given his own establishment in 1756, but insisted on remaining with his mother, and succeeded in appointing Bute as groom of the stole. Bute had already begun to act as adviser to the prince: 'the prospect of serving you and forming your young mind', he wrote, 'is exquisitely pleasing to a heart like mine' (*Letters ... to Lord Bute*, liii). Great hopes were pinned on the young man. In 1758 he gave £50 to John Home, author of the play *Agis*, and visited the performance at Drury Lane three times. Home's dedication to the prince observed that 'the serious cares and princely studies of your youth, the visible tenor of your generous and constant mind, have filled the breasts of all good men with hopes of you'. David Garrick delivered a patriot prologue, drawing the parallel with the Spartan Agis: 'the widow'd mother shewed her parting son, The race of glory which his sire had run'. Mrs Pritchard's epilogue drove the point home— 'France shall yet tremble at the British sword, And dread the vengeance of her ancient Lord' (*The Works of John Home*, ed. H. Mackenzie, 1822 1.185–286). To Bute, George wrote, 'I can't praise enough the noble generous sentiments that run through the whole play' (*Letters ... to Lord Bute*, 9, no. 10).

Bute was savagely handled by contemporaries and has found little favour with historians, but it is to his credit that he established warm personal

relations with the prince where previous governors had notably failed. The prince not merely
responded to Bute's advice, but developed for his
'dearest friend' an unbounded admiration and
affection: 'I esteem your friendship above every
earthly joy', he declared (*Letters ... to Lord Bute*,
38, no. 47). Should Bute set him adrift, he would
renounce the crown and 'retire to some distant
region where in solitude I might for the rest
of my life remain' (ibid., 14, no. 18). This was
romantic and charming, if rather an unrealistic
suggestion from a prince of Wales. There is no
evidence that Bute took advantage of his position to instil autocratic or prerogative notions
into George—nor, indeed, that he possessed them
himself—but he undoubtedly reinforced certain
unfortunate tendencies, towards suspiciousness,
self-righteousness, and a taste for meaningless
melodrama. Far from seeking to subvert the
constitution, he and George saw themselves as
defending it against a possible military coup by
George's uncle, the duke of Cumberland:

> my friend is attacked in the most cruel
> and horrid manner, not for anything he has
> done ... but because he is my friend, and wants
> to see me come to the throne with honor and

not with disgrace, and because he is a friend to the blessed liberties of his country and not to arbitrary notions. (ibid., 3, no. 3)

The merest criticism by Bute—in this case of George's sloth—was enough to plunge him into agonies of remorse. He would throw off that 'incomprehensible indolence, inattention and heedlessness' that Bute had charged him with: 'nothing but the true love you bear me could have led you to remain with me so long' (ibid., 13–14, no. 18).

Bute's plan to eradicate party was easier said than done. In a parliamentary system parties have a remarkable capacity for splitting and re-forming as the great issues change. The early eighteenth-century questions, such as 'the church in danger', were giving way to fresh issues, such as relations with the colonies. In the late 1750s, as George waited for his grandfather to die, the Seven Years' War was fast becoming the domi-nant issue. Though undoubtedly glorious, it was also undeniably expensive, and it involved the career of William Pitt, the organizer of victory. Though formal relations between the prince and the court were maintained—which they had not been under his father or grandfather—George increasingly adopted a political stance, and the reversionary interest gained adherents. In 1755, when Pitt had been dismissed for his attacks upon the duke of Newcastle, he had moved towards an understanding with the prince's circle who gathered at Leicester House. During Pitt's first term as secretary of state under the duke of Devonshire, relations with Bute had remained good. In the summer of 1757, when he came to terms with Newcastle, Pitt wrote to his 'truly noble and generous friend' Bute of the sacrifice he had made in agreeing to work with such a wretch. But as the new coalition ministry established itself and the tide of war began to turn Bute became uneasy, disliking the extent to which Pitt was being pulled into reinforcing Britain's contribution to the war in Germany. By 1758 the prince was talking of the 'infamous and ungrateful part' Pitt was taking, and wrote to Bute that 'he seems to forget that the day will come, when he must expect to be treated according to his deserts' (*Letters...to Lord Bute*, 18–19, nos. 24–5). By 1760 Pitt was 'the blackest of hearts' and 'a true snake in the grass' (ibid., 45, 47, nos. 57, 60). With Legge, the chancellor of the exchequer, the prince was 'incens'd'. Since the prince was also convinced that Henry Fox and Cumberland were 'mirmidons of the blackest kind', planning a military coup, and had no great opinion of Newcastle, the number of leading politicians who did not measure up to his demanding standards was considerable. Luckily he still had Bute: 'in what a pretty pickle I should be in a future day if I had not your sagacious councils' (ibid., 11, no. 14).

Meanwhile, the old king was anxious to see his grandson married before his accession. In 1759 a proposal on behalf of Caroline of Brunswick-Wolfenbüttel was revived; despite George II's assurance that the princess was 'très aimable de toute sa personne', the prince expressed dislike of the pride of petty German courts, and refused (*Letters...to Lord Bute*, 23, no. 30). In 1759 he offered his services in a military capacity, explaining that he would prove 'a terror to the enemy'. Since he had no military experience of any kind the offer was politely deferred, leaving the prince to fume that he was ashamed to be the grandson of George II, to whom he began referring as 'the old man' (ibid., 25, 40–41, nos. 33–4, 49, 51).

As the prince's moment drew near, his aspirations remained extremely vague, but his list of potential victims long and specific. His dependence upon Bute was still total. In November 1759, about to be admitted to the House of Lords, he wrote to Bute: 'I am desirous to know whether I am not to put on my hat on taking my seat' (*Letters...to Lord Bute*, 33, no. 42). The clash with Pitt came on 25 October 1760, the very first day of George III's reign as king of Great Britain and Ireland and elector of Hanover. The declaration to the privy council, drafted by Bute, referred to the 'bloody and expensive war' in progress. Pitt bridled, and the resulting formula—'expensive but just and necessary war' (Brooke, *King George the Third*, 75)—showed how hard it had been to keep the domestic peace. Bute replaced Holdernesse as secretary of state for the north, the new king arguing sensibly that he would otherwise be denounced as a favourite and a minister behind the curtain. The duchess of Northumberland offered a friendly portrait of the new monarch:

He was in his person tall and robust, more graceful than genteel...with an unparalleled air of majestic dignity. There was a noble openness in his countenance, blended with a cheerful good-natured affability. He was fair and fresh coloured and had now and then a few pimples out. His eyes were blue, his teeth extreamly fine. His hair a light auburn...his voice was strong, melodious and clear. (*Diaries of a Duchess*, 35)

At once the search for a suitable bride was resumed. Bute had succeeded late in 1759 in steering George away from Lady Sarah Lennox, Fox's sister-in-law, insisting that he must marry a foreign princess, and the prince, despite incoherent protestations of rapture for Lady Sarah, had himself suggested looking through an almanac for possible German candidates. The princesses of Darmstadt and of Schwedt were ruled out after reports that they were 'stubborn and ill-tempered to the greatest degree' (*Letters...to Lord Bute*, 53, no. 67). The princess of Saxe-Gotha was said to be of a philosophical turn, which George did not relish. In the end, without vast enthusiasm, he settled on Charlotte of Mecklenburg-Strelitz (1744–1818), then aged seventeen. Three separate reports denied her beauty, but she was reputed sensible, and although a Lutheran had no objection to the

Anglican creed. The marriage took place at St James's Palace on 8 September 1761. The bride and groom met at three in the afternoon and were married at nine at night. Horace Walpole, who had not yet learned to despise the king, wrote that he looked 'very handsome, and talked to her continually with great good humour' (Walpole, *Correspondence*, 38.117). A fortnight later, on 22 September 1761, they celebrated their coronation in Westminster Abbey. That year, the king bought Buckingham House (the nucleus of the present Buckingham Palace) and in 1775 he settled it on the queen. It became the usual royal residence in London, all the royal children, save George, being born there.

Parts of the new king's programme were effected with little difficulty. The duke of Newcastle was dismayed to be told that there would be no secret service money for the general election—though in later years George reverted to the practice of his forebears. To bring the tories back into the political fold as a means of eradicating party several of them were appointed to bedchamber posts and tories were welcomed at the levee. But the real author of this policy was Pitt, whose rapprochement with the tories had continued since he took office in 1757. 'The extinction of parties' wrote Horace Walpole, 'had not waited for, but preceded, the dawn of his reign' (Walpole, *Memoirs*, 1.5). Nor were the consequences what the king hoped. The obscuring of party battle lines helped to produce a confused political situation in which ministries came and went in swift succession, and soon parties were re-forming on different principles.

George's determination to appoint Lord Bute and to wind up the war also contributed to the political instability which lasted until Lord North took over as first minister in 1770. From the moment that George succeeded to the throne it was clear that the days of Pitt and Newcastle were numbered. Since one was a national hero and the other commanded a large parliamentary following, and together they had presided over one of the most successful of all administrations, their removal would cause a stir. George was not deterred, since he had Bute on his side. In November 1760 he wrote that unless Pitt behaved, he would 'show him that aversion which will force him to resign', and in September 1761 that 'we must get rid of him in a happier minute than the present one' (*Letters…to Lord Bute*, 50, no. 63; 63, no. 87).

Of the duke of Newcastle, he wrote in April 1762 that 'the more I know of this fellow, the more I wish to see him out of employment' (ibid., 94, no. 129). Pitt obligingly resigned in October 1761 when the cabinet refused to endorse a pre-emptive declaration of war against Spain. Newcastle was at odds with the king, who wished to wind down the German war: in April 1762 George wrote that if Newcastle resigned Bute, 'void of his [Newcastle's] dirty arts', must take the helm (ibid., 93, no. 127). In May 1762 Newcastle went; Bute took his place as first lord of the Treasury and the following day received the Garter. In response to an attack of nerves by Bute, George wrote 'Vigour and the day is ours' (ibid., 109, no. 148).

The Bute ministry

The promotion of Bute and the debate on the peace settlement produced a storm which unnerved Bute and caused the king much uneasiness. Pitt denounced the treaty as inadequate, but Henry Fox was brought in to push it through parliament. Though George was upset at the employment of a man who was, to his mind, associated with corruption and the old gang, Fox did the job, and the treaty was carried in the Commons by 319 votes to 65. But the peace was unpopular. Bute was caricatured as a Scottish favourite, hanged in effigy, assaulted in the streets, and his name was linked with the princess dowager in countless squibs and verses. In this crisis he revealed, as a friend put it, 'more than ordinary sensibility to unmerited reproach and abuse' (J. A. Cannon, *Parliamentary Reform, 1640–1832*, 1973, 58). It was soon his turn to pine for the uninhabited cavern: 'I would retire on bread and water', he wrote in February 1763, 'and think it luxury, compared with what I suffer' (*Lonsdale MSS*, 132). The king tried desperately to dissuade him from retirement but Bute, feeling himself on the brink of a precipice, insisted on resignation. George was most reluctant to accept his suggestion that Henry Fox be offered the Treasury—'in the case of Mr Fox I fear we shall never think alike'—and in the end, without enthusiasm, gave the post to George Grenville (*Letters ... to Lord Bute*, 197, no. 278). The king wrote sadly 'Tho young, I see but too much that there are few very few honest men in this world ... I shall therefore support those who will act for me and without regret change my tools whenever they act contrary to my service' (ibid., 220, no. 309). Yet in his disagreement with Bute over Fox and the earl of Shelburne there were signs that the king, as he gained experience and his marriage prospered, was liberating himself. It was a slow process though, and in the three weeks of April subsequent to Bute's resignation George addressed more than thirty letters to him.

Search for a sound ministry

Grenville's premiership

The Grenville ministry was a nightmare for the king. At an audience on 4 April 1763, George explained to Grenville that he was Bute's choice, and that there must be no negotiation with Newcastle or Pitt—'I would rather quit my Crown' (*Letters...to Lord Bute*, 210, no. 294). There were few disagreements on policy. They agreed on a strong attitude towards the American colonies and were resolved to treat the radical John Wilkes firmly for his attacks on the government in the *North Briton*. But George found Grenville intolerable—unbelievably prolix and much inclined to stand on his dignity. In less than three weeks the king was complaining to Bute of Grenville's 'tiresome manner' and 'ill humour' (ibid., 231, no. 326; 233, no. 328). On 1 June the king asked Bute to sound out Newcastle and his friends, who refused to join the ministry. In August when Egremont, secretary of state and Grenville's brother-in-law, died suddenly Bute was instructed to approach Pitt. At an audience with the king Pitt's demands were unacceptably high and his language lofty—'he saw the boat was sinking, that what he proposed was merely to keep it afloat' (W. J. Smith, 2.199). The breakdown in negotiations left the king stranded, and Grenville resumed office on condition that Bute withdrew completely from active politics. Bute accordingly resigned the last position he retained—that of keeper of the privy purse—and retired to his house at Luton Hoo in Bedfordshire. On 8 September 1763, at the audience, the king told Grenville 'let us not look back, let us only look forward, nothing of that sort shall ever happen again' (ibid., 2.205).

The reconciliation did not last long. By the end of the month Grenville and the king had a sharp exchange over the disposal of the keepership, which the king wanted to give to Sir William Breton, a follower of Bute, and Grenville wanted for himself. The conversation became heated and the king finished with 'Good God! Mr Grenville, am I to be suspected after all I have done?' (W. J. Smith, 2.210). There were reports that Bute had seen William Beckford, Pitt's right-hand man, at Luton, which turned out to be true. These difficulties set the tone for the rest of Grenville's ministry. 'No office fell vacant in any department', wrote the king in a memo, 'that Mr Grenville did not declare he could not serve if the man he recommended did not succeed' (*Correspondence*, ed. Fortescue, 1.164, no. 139). The following year there was another quarrel over the appointment of a successor to William Hogarth as court painter. The king thought Grenville insolent: 'if men presumed to speak to me on business without his leave ... he would not serve an hour' (ibid., 1.164, no. 139). Bute's return to London in the spring of 1764 revived all Grenville's old suspicions, and since Bute's brother, James Stuart Mackenzie, continued to serve as lord privy seal for Scotland, there were further disputes over Scottish patronage.

This constant bickering with his ministers had a serious effect on the king's health and for much of early 1765 he was very unwell. In May he tried once more to escape by appealing through Cumberland to Pitt, but again the great man refused. Grenville and his allies, thinking their position impregnable, imposed severe terms, including the dismissal of Mackenzie, though George pleaded that he had personally promised him the post for life. 'Not able to remove them', wrote the king, 'I could not be so wanting to myself as to treat them otherwise than as Jailers' (*Correspondence*, ed. Fortescue, 1.166, no. 139). The illness produced yet another crisis when the king decided that arrangements for a regency would be prudent. Though the obvious person in the event of the king's death was the queen, George reserved the right to nominate at a later stage. Grenville presumed that this was in order to name the princess dowager and thus restore Bute's influence, though in fact it was because the king did not wish to give the position to his brother the duke of York, whom he thought would be unsuitable. 'My very sleep', the king wrote to Bute, 'is not free from thinking of the men I daily see ... excuse the incoherency of my letter; but a mind ulcer'd by the treatment it meets with from all around is the true cause of it' (*Letters ... to Lord Bute*, 241, no. 336). For a king who had come to the throne determined not to be held in toils, as he insisted his grandfather had been, George was not doing very well. There were demons, at least for the time being, worse than Newcastle and Pitt.

It was inevitable that George III would seek once more to escape from this intolerable situation. The difficulty was that neither Pitt nor Newcastle and his friends were any more willing than Grenville to find themselves in Bute's shadow. In June, despite an audience with the king, Pitt declined once more to come to the rescue, pleading his ally Lord Temple's refusal to take the Treasury. The king consequently authorized Cumberland to begin discussions with Newcastle, and after complicated negotiations the marquess of Rockingham took office as first lord of the Treasury with Newcastle as lord privy seal. Grenville was dismissed at an audience on 10 July 1765, still arguing. He protested that he was utterly ignorant why he had forfeited royal favour, to which the king replied that 'when he had anything proposed to him, it was no longer as counsel, but what he was to *obey*' (W. J. Smith, 3.213).

The Rockingham ministry also expected a similar assurance from the king that 'my lord Bute should not be suffered to interfere in the least degree in any public business whatever' (Bateson, 30–31). They refused categorically to reinstate Mackenzie or to offer him any alternative place. But at least the king had different gaolers.

The Rockingham ministry was not strong and was weakened in October 1765 by the death of its sponsor and supervisor, the duke of Cumberland. Several of its leading members, particularly the duke of Grafton, were anxious to enlist the help of Pitt. Fresh approaches were made in January 1766, but Pitt was ambivalent and unresponsive. In a letter to Bute on 10 January the king made it clear that though he had no great opinion of his ministers' talents, he felt himself committed to support them. He was determined not to negotiate himself with Pitt, 'which I think would for ever stain my name' (*Letters…to Lord Bute*, 245, no. 337). But the main proposal of the ministry, to repeal the Stamp Act, caused great trouble, not only from the hardliners on America, but from those who were concerned at such fluctuations in imperial policy. When some of Bute's friends warned the king that they could not support repeal and tendered their resignations he persuaded them to continue. On 6 February 1766 Bute's intervention in debate in the Lords convinced many that the king was hostile to repeal, and the ministers lost by 59 votes to 54. Rockingham then insisted on authority from

George III that he favoured repeal, and the following day in the Commons the ministry won by
274 votes to 134.

This victory gave a deceptive impression of the
government's strength, and may have made Rockingham over-confident. In April, Grafton told the
king that he had to resign since Pitt would not
join the ministry. Convinced that no alternative
ministry could be formed Rockingham refused to
negotiate either with Pitt or with Bute's former
supporters. Meanwhile Pitt hardened his attitude
towards the administration, with violent denunciations, while his references to Bute and his group
became kinder. At the same time the king's grati-
tude towards the men who had rescued him from
Grenville waned. The duke of Richmond, who
replaced Grafton as secretary of state, was not
a man George liked. On 3 May 1766 the king
wrote to Bute: 'I can neither eat nor sleep: nothing
pleases me but musing on my cruel situation ... if
I am to continue the life of agitation I have these
three years, the next year there will be a Council
of Regency to assist in that undertaking' (ibid.,
248–9, no. 338). In his desperation he swallowed
his pride and approached Pitt once more, and at
an audience on 12 July Pitt agreed to serve.

George's letter to Bute showed how much he had learned: he had parted with the Rockinghams, he wrote, without a quarrel, 'for it is very unpleasant to be afterwards obliged to appear forgetting what one has suffered' (*Letters...to Lord Bute*, 253–4, no. 339). Since the second Earl Temple was again unwilling to serve, Grafton was put in as a nominal first lord of the Treasury, while Pitt, ennobled as Lord Chatham, became lord privy seal and superintending genius. Rockingham and Newcastle went out, but many of the ministers remained. Since Pitt agreed with the king on the paramount need to destroy party, it looked as if, at length, some of the king's youthful hopes were about to be realized. The fifth government in the first six years of his reign took office.

George III certainly bore little blame for the disaster which overcame this ministry. He gave Chatham full and total support, continuing to do so long after it had become apparent that the great man was a broken reed. To Chatham he transferred some of the respect he had felt for Bute. The negotiation to bring in Chatham produced the final breach between the king and Bute, who was greatly hurt that though his brother, James Stuart

Mackenzie, had been restored as lord privy seal for Scotland for life, Bute had not been consulted in the matter by Pitt, and Bute's follower Fletcher Norton had not been given office. He wrote in the autumn of 1766 to beg the king that their private friendship should not be terminated: 'I have for ever done with this bad public, my heart is half broke and my health ruined, with the unmerited barbarous treatment I have received' (*Letters...to Lord Bute*, 256, appx 1). His political following disintegrated, and at last Bute withdrew completely from public life and access to the monarch.

The foundation for a successful ministry appeared to have been laid. Bute's influence was finally removed; an experienced and admired statesman was at the helm who shared the aspirations of the king, and who, in addition, possessed at least in theory, a most exalted view of the dignity of the crown. In fact, the Chatham ministry was one of the greatest political catastrophes in British history. From October 1766 Chatham was stricken by a severe nervous breakdown which rendered him not only incapable of public business but of all human contact. Grafton coped as best he could, but on his appointment had protested that he was unfit to fill the office; he could not deal with America and John Wilkes, and had no control over his effervescent colleague Charles Townshend. Ministers repaired to Chatham when they could obtain permission, only to find him distressingly vague and incoherent. The king treated Chatham with quite remarkable patience. For nine weeks over Christmas 1766 Chatham retired to Bath, and on the way back was marooned at the Castle inn, Marlborough, for another three weeks. When he did reach London in March 1767 the king wrote: 'now you are arrived in town every difficulty will daily decrease' (*Correspondence*, ed. Fortescue, 1.462, no. 490). In fact they multiplied, and Chatham withdrew into complete seclusion, sitting for hours in a darkened room. The restoration of his health must be the only consideration, wrote the king. When in May 1767 Grafton did obtain permission for a visit, George wrote: 'I already look on all difficulties as overcome'. Unfortunately Grafton found Chatham in a pitiful condition, 'nerves and spirits affected to a dreadful degree' (ibid., 1.478, no. 519; *Autobiography … of Grafton*, 136–9). The king offered to visit Chatham, sent him advice on physicians, and constantly encouraged him: 'when you are able to come out all the difficulties that have been encountered will vanish' (*Correspondence*,

ed. Fortescue, 1.491, no. 535). But Chatham did
not come out, and Grafton's problems mounted
with the return of Wilkes as MP for Middlesex in
1768. The king's attitude to Wilkes was uncompro-
mising, despising him as a rake and demagogue
and fearing the power of the mob. 'The expulsion
of Mr Wilkes appears to be very essential and must
be effected', he wrote to North on 25 April 1768;
he urged strong action against the rioters, and in
January 1769 described the expulsion of Wilkes as
'a measure whereon almost my Crown depends'
(ibid., 2.21, no. 613; 2.75, no. 693).

In October 1768 Chatham tendered his resignation. George replied: 'I think I have a right to
insist on your remaining in my service, for I
with pleasure look forward to the time of your
recovery' (ibid., 2.57, no. 669). Chatham insisted
that his health was broken and implored the king
to accept his resignation; should he ever recover
every moment of his life would be devoted to
the king's service. He went, and Grafton sol-
diered on, but there was one last twist. In January
1770, miraculously restored, Chatham reappeared
in the House of Lords, denounced his former colleagues, and declared that his ministry had been

undermined by the baneful influence of the earl of Bute: 'he had been duped when he least suspected treachery…at the time when he was taken ill' (Cobbett, *Parliamentary History*, 16, 1770, 842). His intervention was enough to bring down Grafton's shaky ministry, and the king approached Lord North as a forlorn hope: 'you must easily see that if you do not accept, I have no peer at present…to place in the Duke of Grafton's employment' (*Correspondence*, ed. Fortescue, 2.126, no. 745). As it happened, the years of instability were at an end and George had, at last, backed a winner. North's ministry lasted twelve years, longer than all George's previous ministries put together.

By this time George had changed considerably from the inexperienced youth who had inherited the crown. He was still inclined to censoriousness and though he frequently paid tribute to his own good intentions found it harder to perceive those of others. But the vicissitudes of his first ten years, though highly disagreeable, had left him more circumspect and more inclined to distance himself. Villains had become saviours, and saviours villains, in bewildering combinations. Bute, once a man of unsurpassed wisdom, had, in the end, seemed much like other politicians; Henry Fox, whom George despised as a man of corruption, had had to be employed to carry the peace; his uncle Cumberland, the ogre of George's Leicester House days, had saved him from Grenville. Pitt had moved from a scoundrel in the 1750s into a mentor and friend in the 1760s, only to revert to 'that perfidious man' in the 1770s (*Correspondence*, ed. Fortescue, 4.59, no. 2224). Not surprisingly, the king told North in 1778: 'I have had enough of personal negotiations' (ibid., 4.58, no. 2221). The reign of virtue had not been abandoned but it would be a long road.

Family, Lord North, and America

Children and siblings

As well as being head of state George became, on the death of his grandfather, head of the royal family. With his mother, the princess dowager, he remained on cordial terms, and the misunderstanding over her initial exclusion from the Regency Bill was the last straw in his relations with Grenville. His marriage to Charlotte proved both affectionate and—as George had fervently hoped—fruitful. The queen preferred a quiet domestic life, shared her husband's love of music, and had no wish to play a political role. For the first time since the reign of Charles I there were no mistresses at court to complicate private or public matters. Their first son, George (later George IV) was born after eleven months of married life on 12 August 1762, and was followed by eight more sons and six daughters, the last, Amelia, born in 1783. By May 1770, when Elizabeth was born, there were seven children in the royal nursery. The king was an affectionate father: when Prince Octavius died in 1783 at the age of four, George declared 'There will be no Heaven for me if Octavius is not there' (*The Correspondence of George, prince of Wales*, 1.108n). It is doubtful whether the king read widely, particularly in later life when his eyesight was giving trouble, but his long audiences with Dr Johnson, James Beattie, Charles Burney, and others suggest a cultivated mind and a gift for pleasant conversation. To Johnson he paid an elegant compliment, and his remark—no doubt obvious enough—that Johnson ought to attempt a literary history bore fruit in the most delightful of Johnson's works, the *Lives of the Poets*.

The king's siblings provided a variety of problems. At the accession his brother Edward was twenty-one, William seventeen, Henry fifteen, and Frederick ten; his elder sister Augusta was twenty-three, Louisa eleven, and Caroline nine. His sister Elizabeth, a bright girl, who had been born with a deformity, had died of appendicitis in 1759 at the age of eighteen; his brother Frederick died of tuberculosis in 1765. Prince Edward, once his favourite companion, became a cause of anxiety. His way of life was raffish and self-indulgent, he showed signs of dabbling in opposition politics, and in May 1767 was said to be 'in great disgrace at court' (Walpole, *Correspondence*, 22.524). He died suddenly in Monaco in September 1767. Princess Augusta, the king's eldest sister, married in January 1764 Charles, duke of Brunswick, but her husband was unfaithful, the marriage did not prosper, and by 1765 Rigby reported 'their living very ill together' (*Correspondence of … Bedford*, 3.318). Another sister, Louisa, small and pretty, died of tuberculosis in May 1768. The king's troubles continued in the 1770s. Henry, duke of Cumberland, his third brother, was successfully sued for damages in 1770 over his relations with Lady Grosvenor, and his fervent but ungrammatical love letters were read out in court. In January 1772 came news that George's youngest sister, Caroline, married to Christian VII of Denmark, had been arrested for adultery and her lover executed; though George negotiated for her an honourable retirement to Celle, she died in 1775. The princess dowager died in February 1772 after a long and painful cancer of the throat. Disentangled from

Lady Grosvenor the duke of Cumberland hastily made a secret marriage to Anne Horton, a widow, and was told bluntly by the king that he had 'irretrievably ruined himself' (Brooke, *King George the Third*, 273). To prevent any repetition of such *mésalliances* the king insisted on the passage of the Royal Marriages Act in 1772, which forbade the marriage of any member of the royal family under twenty-five without the monarch's approval. No sooner had this become law than the duke of Gloucester, to whom the king had confided his outrage at Cumberland's behaviour, confessed that he had been secretly married for the past six years to Lady Waldegrave, an illegitimate daughter of Sir Edward Walpole. Neither duchess was ever received at court. At times the king must have turned with relief to politics.

North and the America crisis

Until overwhelmed by the American troubles, Lord North's ministry gave the king some respite from political difficulties. North and George were on good terms, and the prime minister was given the Garter within eighteen months. Government majorities were quickly restored, opposition withered, the Wilkes issue was defused, and war with

Spain, which would have brought a demand for the recall of Chatham, averted. The king was content to play a less prominent political role, following North's lead: 'you are my sheet anchor', he wrote in November 1775 (*Correspondence*, ed. Fortescue, 3.279, no. 1742).

By that time the waves were rolling high again. The origin of the American crisis lay in the cost of the Seven Years' War, which made it imperative for ministers to raise more revenue from the colonists. It is possible that the repeal of the Stamp Act, though accompanied by the Declaratory Act reaffirming parliamentary authority, might have averted a clash, had not Charles Townshend, during Chatham's illness, rekindled agitation with his miscellaneous duties. The defeat of the government's land tax proposals in February 1767— 'a thing almost unknown in Parliament'—by an opposition led by Grenville made it all the more urgent to raise additional revenue from America (*Correspondence*, ed. Fortescue, 1.453, no. 473). Townshend's sudden death in September 1767 meant that the problem passed to North. Although his own instincts were conciliatory, he had little room for manoeuvre, since parliament, beset by Wilkite rioters at home and organized resistance in the colonies, was in no mood to truckle to violence. Two months after taking office in 1770 North proposed to withdraw the Townshend duties, 'which had given umbrage to the Americans', retaining only a small tax on tea at 3*d*. in the pound (Cobbett, *Parliamentary History*, 16, 1770, 853). He had some difficulty in persuading his followers to agree. The gesture lost much of its point since the same day the Boston massacre took place, inflaming American opinion. In June 1772 American patriots seized the revenue cutter *Gaspée*, wounded the captain, and burnt the ship. In 1773 the Boston Tea Party, accompanied by the tarring and feathering of a customs officer, persuaded most Britons that the Americans were incorrigible. Even the friends of America, Chatham and Rockingham, condemned the outrage and agreed that Britain must protect its officials and their property. The decision to close the port of Boston as a reprisal passed without opposition.

Since it was the view of almost all members of parliament that strong measures should be taken against the colonists, it is not surprising to find the king taking a similar line. In *Common Sense*, Tom Paine denounced him as 'the royal brute', and the Declaration of Independence credited him with a settled plan to enslave his American subjects. In fact, until the crisis, like most Britons, he showed little interest in America. Once resistance flared he insisted that it was his duty to uphold the authority of the imperial parliament: 'I am fighting the battle of the legislature', he wrote, 'therefore have a right to expect an almost unanimous support' (*Correspondence*, ed. Fortescue, 3.256, no. 1709). When the Americans co-ordinated their resistance in the summer of 1774 through the Philadelphia Congress, his attitude hardened. 'The New England governments are in a state of rebellion', he wrote in November 1774: 'blows must decide whether they are to be subject to this country or independent' (ibid., 3.153, no. 1556). It is not easy to see what other attitude a constitutional monarch could have adopted, even setting aside the improbability that an eighteenth-century ruler would be sympathetic towards rebels.

Once rioting developed into warfare after the first shots at Lexington in April 1775, the king took little part in strategic discussions, though he was greatly exercised in raising and reviewing troops and building men-of-war. His main contribution was to stiffen the resolve of his ministers, retain the important services of Lord North, and head off any negotiations with the parliamentary opposition. After the first severe setback in October 1777, when General Burgoyne surrendered at Saratoga, North warned the king that 'some material change of system' was needed, and that a national coalition might be necessary (*Correspondence*, ed. Fortescue, 3.504, no. 2095). The following month he complained that the disaster had deprived him of his memory and understanding, and confessed his own incapacity for the office he held. In February North begged leave to approach Chatham as 'of all the opposition, the person who would be of most service to his Majesty' (ibid., 4.38, no. 2193). George III was extremely reluctant: 'No advantage to this country nor personal danger can ever make me address myself for assistance either to Lord Chatham or any other branch of the opposition honestly I would rather lose the crown I now wear than bear the ignominy of possessing it under their shackles' (ibid., 4.59, no. 2221). He was forced to agree to an approach, but added: 'I do not expect Lord Chatham and his crew will come to your assistance' (ibid.). Chatham, as usual, insisted on an audience and demanded full powers. The king refused to have him as

'Dictator', and hinted to North that he could find himself Chatham's first victim. In a phrase that might have recalled Bute, North retorted that capital punishment would be better than the mental agony he suffered. From this dilemma both men were rescued by news of Chatham's final collapse in the House of Lords on 7 April 1778. The king was too honest to pretend to grief he did not possess: 'may not the political exit of Lord Chatham', he enquired briskly of North the following day, 'encline you to continue at the head of my affairs?' (ibid., 4.102, no. 2284).

Though the danger from Chatham had gone North still pined for release, particularly when the parliamentary session drew near or the news from America was bad. The entry into the war of France and Spain in 1778 and 1779, though making it more popular, placed an enormous strain on the country's resources, particularly its naval strength. Opposition in parliament, though few in numbers, was vigorous and highly personal: Edmund Burke was not the only member to threaten North with impeachment and the block. Under these circumstances retaining his first minister was a major consideration for the king, since

North's conciliatory attitude and parliamentary skill were valuable assets. George paid off his minister's personal debts in 1777 and for some years kept up a private correspondence with Charles Jenkinson and John Robinson, who monitored the first minister's state of mind. This has been seen as a sinister example of backstairs influence and each man acquired a reputation for intrigue, but since the arrangement was intended not to undermine North but to encourage and support him, it appears scarcely objectionable. Nor did the king flinch from emotional blackmail: 'are you resolved, agreeable to the example of the Duke of Grafton', he wrote to North in the spring of 1778, 'at the hour of danger to desert me?' (*Correspondence*, ed. Fortescue, 4.72, no. 2240).

It has often been suggested that by his obstinacy George III protracted the American war. But no eighteenth-century ruler would contemplate tamely surrendering the greater part of his empire, nor is it clear why Frederick the Great's resistance in the Seven Years' War should be regarded as heroic, yet George's resistance in America foolhardy. Until after Yorktown it was not certain that the outcome must be defeat.

As late as 1781 there was mutiny in the American army, and George Washington wrote that there was 'not a single farthing in the military chest' (*The Writings of George Washington*, ed. J. C. Fitzpatrick, 39 vols., 1931–44, 21.55); in France, Vergennes conceded that it was 'a war of hard cash, and if we drag it out, the last shilling may not be ours' (Mackesy, 386). Admiral Rodney's great naval victory off the Saints in 1782, and General Elliott's magnificent defence of Gibraltar enabled better terms of peace to be obtained than had seemed likely.

America lost, political turmoil

After Yorktown the king's resolve held but North's parliamentary majority melted away, until on 15 March 1782, on a vote of no confidence, it stood at only nine. Even then the king was most unwilling to contemplate a change of ministry. 'If you resign before I have decided what I will do', he warned North, 'you will certainly for ever forfeit my regard' (*Correspondence*, ed. Fortescue, 5.397, no. 3567). North reminded the king sharply:

The torrent is too strong to be resisted; Your Majesty is well apprized that, in this country, the Prince on the Throne, cannot, with prudence, oppose the deliberate resolution of the House of Commons... Your Majesty having persevered, as long as possible, in what you thought right, can lose no honour if you yield at length. (ibid., 5.395, no. 3566)

The crisis which followed was as painful to the king as those of the 1760s. He drafted an abdication speech expressing his sorrow that he 'finds he can be of no further utility to his native country', and declaring his intention to retire to Hanover (ibid., 5.425, no. 3601). It was never delivered. He was obliged to accept Rockingham, leader of the largest opposition group, but installed the earl of Shelburne, the least objectionable of his opponents, as a check and counter-balance to the new first minister. He was forced to agree not only to recognition of American independence, but to the programme of economical reform to which the new ministers were pledged.

The influence of the crown, which Lord Dunning's motion of 1780 had declared to be increasing, was more the influence of government than of the monarchy itself. Nevertheless, the king was deeply offended at the proposal to reform his household by act of parliament. Ministers conceded that the household should be reformed by internal regulation and the king sent a message to parliament to that effect. A number of sinecure officers such as the master of the stag hounds and the master of the harriers were abolished, but the effect was slight, and one unforeseen consequence was an enhancement in the importance of honours.

A struggle for power between Shelburne and Rockingham began in the first week of the new ministry and continued until the latter's death on 1 July 1782. The king gave Shelburne full support, grooming him for the succession, and at once invited him to form an administration. Charles James Fox, the second secretary of state, and a number of his colleagues resigned, protesting that they could not serve under Shelburne. The balance between the contending factions was held by Lord North, who had retained a sizeable following. Despite his parting protestations of devotion to the king's service, his decision depended primarily upon the terms of the peace treaty which Shelburne was negotiating, and the nature of the approaches made to him by the other two parties. In August the king, anxious to buttress Shelburne's position before parliament met, addressed a personal appeal to North, begging him to give 'the most cordial support' to Shelburne's ministry and to use his great influence with the country gentlemen (*Correspondence*, ed. Fortescue, 6.97, no. 3872). North's reply was circumspect, provoking the king to remark that loyalty did not last long. When the terms of the settlement became known the neglect of the American loyalists made it very difficult for North to advise acceptance, he closed with Fox's offer of a coalition, and in February 1783 Shelburne was forced to resign.

George was distracted at the thought of once more employing Charles James Fox, whom he despised on both personal and public grounds, as the son of Henry Fox, as a gambler and a libertine, an evil influence on the prince of Wales, and a politician whose avowed aim was to strike 'a good stout blow' at the influence of the crown. His abdication speech was brought out and revised. For six weeks he refused to surrender to the coalition, until the total absence of an alternative ministry obliged him to yield. The third duke of Portland became first minister, Fox and North the secretaries of state. He had been forced to give way, the king told the third Earl Temple, to:

> the most unprincipled coalition the annals of this or any other nation can equal. I have withstood it till not a single man is willing to come to my assistance ... I trust the eyes of the nation will soon be opened as my sorrow may prove fatal to my health if I remain long in this thraldom. (*Correspondence*, ed. Fortescue, 6.329–30, no. 4272)

The coalition ministry was living on borrowed time. The king retired into sulky seclusion, refusing to grant peerages as a demonstration of hostility. A very sharp dispute over the proposed allowance for the prince of Wales nearly brought about a crisis. George thought the provision suggested by the ministers was far too lavish and expressed his 'utter indignation and astonishment' at this attempt to 'gratify the passions of an ill-advised young man ... the public shall know how well founded the principles of economy are in those who have so loudly preached it up' (Cannon, *Fox–North Coalition*, 96). Fox and his friends prepared to 'die handsomely' (ibid., 97), but Temple and others advised the king that a family dispute was not a good issue for a public showdown. The king made a sudden retreat, apologizing profusely to Portland, and explaining that the American war had 'soured and ruined his temper' (ibid., 98).

King George and Pitt the Younger

The rise of the Younger Pitt

The pivotal position in the ministerial crisis of autumn 1783 was that of young William Pitt, who had been sounded out in the spring, but had declined to form a ministry. Ironically, this meant that the king's hopes of rescue depended upon the Grenvilles—since Temple was Pitt's first cousin and the son of George Grenville—the very people he had detested in the 1760s. But one difficulty was that the king was uncertain to what extent Pitt felt himself pledged to further measures of economical reform and to parliamentary reform—his maiden speech in 1781 had, after all, been made on the need to reduce the influence of the crown. The opportunity for which the king had waited came with the decision of ministers to bring forward an India Bill, yet another attempt to frame an adequate administrative structure for the vast territories which could no longer be left to the unchecked rule of the East India Company. Since any proposal must involve intervention in the company's affairs and could be represented as an invasion of its charter, there was bound to be scope for powerful opposition. The duke of Manchester, a coalition supporter to whom the outlines of the scheme were sent in September 1783, saw at once the potential political danger:

His Majesty perhaps might be induced to acquiesce without being thoroughly convinced of the fitness of the measure, and should he coldly support it in the outset, means at the same time might be found to thwart it before it could be brought to maturity. (*Eighth Report*, Historical Manuscripts Commission, 2.134)

George III seems to have offered no objection to the draft, and the bill passed the Commons with a comfortable majority of 229 votes to 120. Unless the king intervened the bill would almost certainly go through the Lords without difficulty. On 1 December Thurlow, lord chancellor until 1782, acting in conjunction with Temple, had an audience in which he suggested that the king should make his disapproval of the bill known. But any alternative ministry would still need a Commons leader, for whom North, Fox, Burke, and Richard Sheridan would prove formidable adversaries. In a secret negotiation authorized by the king, Pitt agreed to serve, provided that 'the Great Patriot's' hostility to the bill was made clear. In an audience with Temple, the king declared that 'whoever votes in the House of Lords for the India Bill is not *his* friend' (*Abergavenny MSS*, 62). Amid scenes of great excitement the bill was rejected by 87 votes to 79. Three days later Fox, North, and Portland, at a midnight conclave, received from the king terse notices of dismissal, 'as audiences on such occasions must be unpleasant' (*Correspondence*, ed. Fortescue, 6.476, no. 4546).

Pitt took office in a minority administration, with Temple as his secretary of state. On 17 December a motion that to report any opinion of the monarch in order to influence voting was a 'high crime and misdemeanour' was carried in the Commons by 153 votes to 80 (*Journals of the House of Commons*, 39, 1783, 842). Temple's resignation after only three days was a blow which nearly shattered the enterprise at the outset, and George wrote that he felt himself on the edge of a precipice. But the Christmas recess gave the chance for Pitt and his friends to proselytize. The engines of patronage were turned on: 'they are crying peerages about the streets in barrows', wrote Horace Walpole, with pardonable exaggeration (Walpole, *Correspondence*, 33.430). By the time parliament reassembled in January 1784 the coalition's majority was down to 39. The king urged a dissolution: 'we must be men; and if we mean to save the country, we must cut those threads that cannot be unravelled. Half measures are ever puerile' (Stanhope, 1.appx, v). Again he threatened to abdicate. The ministers struggled on, and on 8 March the coalition's majority was down to one vote—191 against 190. The king recognized the significance of the figures. Pitt's letter conveying the news was, he wrote, 'the most satisfactory I have received for many months': Pitt would 'be ever able to reflect with satisfaction that in having supported me he has saved the Constitution, the most perfect of human formations' (ibid., 1.appx, x). The subsequent general election endorsed the king's detestation of the coalition and placed Pitt firmly in power. The results, wrote the king, were 'more favourable than the most sanguine could have expected' (ibid., 1.appx, xii).

After two years of turmoil the king was once more in clear waters.

53

The loss of America, finally acknowledged in September 1783, though a humiliating blow, had compensating advantages. Britain's economic and financial recovery was remarkably swift, and the disappearance of the American problem removed a factor which had unsettled the political scene since the earliest years of George III's reign. To the new American ambassador, John Adams, the king managed to give a dignified welcome in June 1785:

> I will be free with you. I was the last to consent to the separation; but the separation having been made and having become inevitable, I have always said, as I say now, that I would be the first to meet the friendship of the United States as an independent power. (*Works of John Adams*, 8.255–7)

Pitt held office for the next sixteen years, and by the time he resigned in 1801 the king was an elderly man in uncertain health. Relations between the two were correct rather than cordial, but each understood that he depended on the other. It was clear to Pitt how greatly the absence of the king's confidence had weakened the coalition ministry, while the king realized that only Pitt could hold Charles James Fox at bay. There were, of course, occasional disagreements, sometimes sharp, and some residual suspicion on both sides to be removed. The king regretted Pitt's continued commitment to parliamentary reform, and when the issue came up in 1785 Pitt was concerned lest his own position be undermined by secret influence: 'there is but one issue of the business', he warned the king, 'to which he could look as fatal ... that is the possibility of the measure being rejected by the weight of those who were supposed to be connected with government' (*Later Correspondence of George III*, 1.139, no. 182). George III assured him that, though he disapproved of the measure, he had kept his opinion to himself, but added 'there are questions men will not by friendship be biased to accept' (Barnes, 203). Nothing could save Pitt's bill, fewer than half the placemen voted with him, and he went down to defeat by 248 votes to 174. Though it was a mortification, Pitt's government was in no danger. George's note acknowledging Pitt's account of the debate shows how tactful he could sometimes be. Ignoring the subject matter, he passed on Lord Camden's opinion that Pitt's speech had been 'a masterly performance' (Stanhope, 1.appx, xvii). The most cogent and scholarly attempt to establish that Pitt was in thrall to the king has not won widespread support (Barnes). There was no dramatic change in the constitutional relationship betwen the king and his first minister, but certain long-term factors were beginning to operate against the personal supervision of the monarch—the growing complexity of public business, the growth of party allegiance, the expansion of public opinion, and the development of cabinet solidarity. In addition, a factor which had strengthened George's position in the 1760s—his youth and expectations— no longer operated: in the 1780s his prime minister was in his twenties, while the king was approaching fifty and had a grown-up son.

The prince of Wales

That son, George, prince of Wales, was, with his brothers, a source of great anxiety to the king. It had not been easy to find governors for the prince and his brother Frederick, and they had not been very successful: one of them, Lord Holdernesse, had been reduced by illness to taking a long recuperation abroad before resigning in 1776, explaining that he had not obtained that share of the princes' confidence which would enable him to be of use. In August 1780 the king had written to the prince that he had not made the progress in his studies that had been anticipated, and begging him to lead a devout and decent life. But the prince had already made considerable progress in other respects. In 1779 he had persuaded Perdita Robinson, the actress, to become his mistress. She had extracted from him a guarantee of £20,000 when he succeeded, and in 1781 was threatening to print his love letters, written under the signature Florizel. Apprised of the affair, the king had to find £5000 to redeem the letters, adding, characteristically, 'I am happy at being able to say that I never was personally engaged in such a transaction' (*Correspondence*, ed. Fortescue, 5.269, no. 3396). The prince immediately plunged into another affair with a Mme Hardenberg, confessing to his brother that he was spitting blood and thought his brain would split. The injured husband took his wife off to Brussels. The following month the prince wrote to his brother that 'the king is excessively cross and ill-tempered, and uncommonly grumpy' (*Correspondence of George, Prince of Wales*, 1.73, no. 50). The prince's political attachment to Fox and the dispute in

The prince's lavish lifestyle ensured that he was
well provided with debt. The acrimonious settlement of 1783 had paid off £23,000, and given him
the use of Carlton House. The prince promised
instant reformation and the king total forgive-
ness. The prince at once commenced large-scale
alterations to Carlton House, ran once more into
debt, and declared in the spring of 1784 that
he would be obliged to live abroad. From the
'unruly passions' of his son, complained the king,
'every absurdity and impropriety may be expected'
(*Later Correspondence of George III*, 1.85, no. 114).
The king was forced to send urgently to Brighton,
as a father and a sovereign, to forbid the prince
from leaving the country. The prince's debts, he
remarked, amounted to £100,000, 'which in one
year and without gaming seems hardly credible'
(ibid., 1.89, no. 120). A further reason for the
prince's continental plans was that he had fallen
madly in love with a widow, Mrs Fitzherbert, and
was determined to follow her to the Netherlands
and marry her. Under the terms of the Act of
Settlement this would forfeit his succession to the
throne, and by the Royal Marriages Act it would

be invalid. In July 1784, in a frenzy of passion, he had stabbed himself, not very deeply.

George III was already in financial difficulties, partly because of his growing family, partly because he had taken on an election debt of £23,000 incurred during Lord North's ministry. Colonel Hotham, the prince's treasurer, was asked to make a new assessment of the prince's debts, a task which he confessed to be impossible: at a rough estimate they had reached £150,000. To compound his difficulties and after abandoning a scheme to escape to America, the prince went through a secret marriage in December 1785 with Mrs Fitzherbert, conducted by a clergyman set free from the Fleet prison for the occasion. The following year he purchased a farmhouse at Brighton and began building the Pavilion. By that time his debts had reached £270,000, which he attributed to the 'incompetency' of his income. In 1787 the whole question was laid before parliament, which voted £161,000 for redemption of debt and £60,000 for the completion of Carlton House. When a member raised the matter of the prince's marriage, Fox, speaking on personal authority, declared the rumours quite untrue. The

Family life

The prince's brothers, Frederick and William, were aged twenty-one and nineteen in 1784. Frederick had been placed in the army, despite the fact that from the age of six months he had been bishop of Osnabrück, and was serving in Germany. He shared his brother's pursuit of women and was addicted to gambling, but had more sense and understood the damage which a public rift would do to the royal family. Prince William was in the navy. Frederick reported from Hanover that he was given to swearing, a habit he retained, and did not much care how he behaved. In August 1784, the king wrote to reproach him for 'forecastle' manners and his love of improper company (*Later Correspondence of George III*, 1.77, no. 104). The four youngest princes were too young to have started to run up debt. The princesses lived quiet lives under the watchful eye of Queen Charlotte. In 1791 the princess royal, still unmarried at twenty-five, confided to the prince of Wales 'the tiresome and confined life' she was forced to live, and the 'violence and caprice of her mother's temper'. Any marriage would be 'preferable to the misery she was a slave to at present' (*Correspondence of George, Prince of Wales*, 2.162, no. 591). In 1797 she accepted an offer from the duke of Württemberg, lived in Germany, and never saw her father again.

George's court was sober and respectable. The king and queen were good Anglicans, and paid attention to their religious duties without ostentation. Fanny Burney has left a vivid description of the formality and punctiliousness of court life. The king was not fond of St James's, Kensington, or Hampton Court palaces, and had purchased Buckingham House to develop as a family residence. For country air he used Kew Palace or Windsor, which he increasingly enjoyed. 'I certainly see as little of London as I possibly can', he wrote in 1785, 'and am never a volunteer there' (Brooke, *King George the Third*, 287). Audiences, correspondence, and the levees took up much of his time. He enjoyed riding and hunting, preferred family dinners to entertaining, visited the theatre and concerts regularly, and enjoyed cards and domestic music in the evenings. His preference for frugal meals and his sober habits became a source of fun for the graphic satirists.

One of the remarkable features of George's way of life was his comparative lack of interest in travel. He never visited his Hanoverian dominions, though they were, at least in theory, very dear to him. He gloried in the name of Britain, but knew little about it. Scotland, Wales, and Ireland were ignored. So was most of England. The royal family visited Weymouth for sea bathing, and when at Cheltenham in 1788, the king and queen saw Gloucester, Worcester, Tewkesbury, and a few nearby manor houses like Matson and Croome. But the midlands and north were a closed book, as was the south-west and Cornwall. He never visited the University of Cambridge, nor the great cathedrals at York, Lincoln, Norwich, or Wells. The explanation seems to be a certain lack of intellectual vitality, the problem of conveying court and family, and the king's preference for a routine and familiar existence.

Illness, revolution, and war

The Regency crisis

The king's pleasant and relatively undemanding way of life was shattered late in 1788 by the onset of a severe illness. Physically strong, abstemious in diet and conduct, taking regular exercise, George was often agitated by political difficulties, his opinions strongly held and frequently expressed with vigour. John Brooke and other historians have denied that there were any traces of derangement in his illness of 1765, though on 18 March George Grenville noted 'the king's countenance and manner a good deal estranged' (W. J. Smith, 3.122). This may have been caused, or at least exacerbated, by the presence of Grenville himself, whom the king disliked intensely. But the king's determination, once he had recovered, to make provision for a regency suggests that his indisposition was severe. At other periods he was much agitated: in 1783 William Grenville reported him highly excited and talking incessantly. The 1788 illness began in the summer with unpleasant stomach pain. The visit to Cheltenham, though a great success socially, did not put an end to it. By October the king was seriously unwell, sleeping badly, hoarse with relentless talking, unsteady on his feet, mentally confused, and occasionally violent. These alarming symptoms lost nothing in the retelling. In December Dr Francis Willis, a mad-doctor, was brought in; his implements included a strait-jacket and a restraining chair—which the king referred to ruefully as his 'coronation chair'. The king's conversation was at times indecent, he declared a violent passion for Lady Pembroke, and talked against the queen.

The political implications of the king's illness were dramatic. If the incapacity became permanent the prince of Wales must become regent. In that case he would certainly dismiss William Pitt and install in office Charles James Fox and the remnants of the coalition. The opposition insisted that the regent should have full powers, including the granting of peerages. Pitt and his friends argued that, certainly at first, the regent's powers should be limited and defined. A number of government supporters, among them Thurlow, prepared to shuffle. The piquancy of the reversal of roles, Pitt arguing for parliamentary sanctions, Fox for the prince's prerogative, was not lost on observers. A further complication was that the Irish House of Commons rebelled against the lord lieutenant and addressed the prince to assume the government at once. The prospect of the component parts of the British Isles moving in different directions, as Scotland and England had briefly done in the 1700s, began to loom. But on 17 February 1789, three days before the Regency Bill was due to take effect, it was announced that the king was convalescent. A thanksgiving service was held at St Paul's on 23 April and medals were struck commemorating George IIIs recovery.

The nature of the king's illness was much discussed. Of the severe mental disturbance, albeit intermittent, there can be no doubt, and the treatment of lunatics in that period was so brutal that the king's fears and resentments are easily understood. The contemporary explanation by the medical consultants was old fashioned and bizarre: George's condition was, in their opinion, caused by a 'humour' in the legs, which the king's own imprudence (omitting to change wet stockings) 'drove from thence into the bowels' (Buckingham, 2.6–7). Nineteenth-century historians, few of them sympathetic to the king, were content to accept his illness as lunacy, either an inherited defect or the result of external pressures. In the 1920s, under the influence of Freud, it became fashionable to regard the derangement as the product of severe sexual repression, and the king's attitude to Lady Pembroke and the queen was deemed peculiarly significant. In 1969 Ida Macalpine and Richard Hunter pointed out that many of the symptoms, particularly purple urine, suggested that the illness was porphyria, a rare but acknowledged hereditary illness, which often produces neurological damage and mental instability.

The consequences of the illness were considerable. It did little good for the opposition, some of whom, like Edmund Burke, had expressed their case extravagantly, appearing to gloat over the king's condition. The prospect of a return to power by Fox and his friends sobered a number of people. The rift between the Irish and British parliaments meant that the possibility of a union, mooted after the beginning of Grattan's parliament in 1782, moved to the forefront of people's minds, and especially that of Pitt. But most marked was a great rise in the reputation and standing of the king himself. The 'Farmer George' image and the 'Father of his People' description gained greater popularity in this period, and newspapers, circulating more widely than ever before, began to devote increasing space to stories and anecdotes about him. In part this was the natural result of pity, reinforced by the contrast between the homely virtues of the king and the self-indulgence of the prince. But the change preceded his illness. On their visit to Cheltenham the royal family had been gratified at the large and enthusiastic crowds which turned out to welcome them. George III had shaken off the burden of Hanover, which had dogged his grandfather and great-grandfather. He was the first king in living memory whose domestic life was beyond reproach. His stand against the Americans, which won him few friends among nineteenth-century liberal historians, was popular with most of his subjects, who disliked the ambivalent attitude of the opposition towards national defeats. One result of the loss of America, though short-lived, was to foster a mood of insularity and conservatism, which could easily identify with the king. He also gained great applause for the composure he showed on several occasions when his life was in danger—when stabbed by Margaret Nicholson in 1786, stoned in the state coach on his way to parliament in the dark days of 1795, or shot at by James Hadfield at Drury Lane Theatre in 1800.

Such a severe illness, and his advancing years, were bound to reduce the king's political activity. For some time afterwards he complained of tiredness, and on 23 February 1789 he wrote to Pitt that for the remainder of his days he would 'only keep that superintending eye which can be effected without labour or fatigue' (Stanhope, 2.appx, vii). But, as Pitt soon discovered, that eye remained vigilant, and within days the king was writing to remind him to see to the translation of the bishop of Gloucester to St Asaph. The number of court days was reduced and the royal family henceforth took regular holidays at Weymouth. There was less necessity for the king's intervention since on most issues he saw eye to eye with Pitt, and the ministry was securely established. At the general election of June 1790 the opposition lost ground: it did not divide on the address in November 1790, and in December, in the division on the Spanish convention, it was beaten by 123 votes to 247. Pitt's authority within his cabinet was unchallenged. In May 1792, when relations between him and Lord Chancellor Thurlow broke down, the prime minister wrote simply that the king must choose between them. Despite the 'affection' (ibid., 2.150) he felt for Thurlow, George had no hesitation in dismissing him.

Meanwhile developments in revolutionary France were taking place which shaped the rest of George III's reign. The most immediate effect was to weaken Fox and the opposition still further, as first Burke, then Loughborough, and finally Portland and Windham moved over to support the government. In March 1792 came an echo from the past when the king coolly acknowledged the news of Lord Bute's death. Embarrassed at his youthful infatuation, George ultimately wrote it out of his mind, confiding to George Rose in 1804 that at his accession Bute had insisted on taking office, much against the king's will. The events of the French Revolution, which many in Britain had watched at first with detached interest and some satisfaction, became menacing with the execution of Louis XVI and Marie Antoinette in 1793 and the declaration of war by the French. The king denounced the executions as the work of savages and welcomed war against 'that unprincipled country whose aim at present is to destroy the foundations of every civilised state' (*Later Correspondence of George III*, 2.xiv). But though he followed the progress of the war with great attention and offered suggestions, the king's role was not central, nor did Pitt need the constant encouragement that North had sought twenty years earlier.

The king's children: marriages and mistresses

One problem which did not abate was that of George III's family. Indeed, almost the first communications George received after his recovery in 1789 were from princes Frederick and William warning him of the inadequacy of the financial provision made for them: 'I think it my duty not to incur the risk of deceiving Your Majesty', wrote the latter, 'by giving expectations that I can live within the present income' (*Later Correspondence of George III*, 1.417, no. 518). The conduct of the prince of Wales and of Prince Frederick during their father's illness had been very equivocal and relations afterwards were strained. A meeting with the king passed off without mishap, but political and public questions were studiously avoided. In 1791 Prince Frederick married the princess royal of Prussia. The princess royal of Britain was safely married in 1797 to the duke of Württemberg, though she was dismayed at seeing him, since he was even fatter than the prince of Wales, who was a mere 17 stone.

The rest of the royal princes provided excellent copy for the more scurrilous newspapers. Lord Melbourne, explaining their behaviour to the young Queen Victoria, blamed it on the Royal Marriages Act, which 'sent them like so many wild beasts into society, making love everywhere they went, and then saying that they were very sorry they couldn't marry them' (*Later Correspondence of George III*, 2.xxxviii). Prince William settled down with Mrs Jordan, a popular actress, and began producing a large family of Fitz-Clarences; his offer of naval service during the war was politely declined. Prince Edward (eventually father of the future Queen Victoria), confessed in 1787 a substantial debt and like his brothers promised immediate reformation; it did not last and he was subjected to one of the king's, by now, routine letters of reproach. He then found a French lady, Mme de St Laurent, and set up home with her. Prince Augustus Frederick was of a more serious cast of mind and was said to be contemplating holy orders. But in December 1793 a gentleman giving his name as Mr Augustus Frederick and dressed 'like a common shopkeeper' was privately married at St George's, Hanover Square, to an eight-months pregnant Lady Augusta Murray. This impenetrable disguise sufficed for a whole month, until *The Times* revealed the marriage of 'a young gentleman of very high rank' to 'the daughter of a northern peer'. The marriage was declared void in July 1794 under the terms of the Royal Marriages Act.

Meanwhile the behaviour of the prince of Wales was so hard to defend that it would have threatened Pitt's large parliamentary majority had not the opposition had its own reasons for palliating his conduct. By 1795 his debts had reached £630,000, and since friends could no longer oblige and bankers were unwilling to make loans, the only escape was into matrimony, which would enable a fresh application to be made to parliament. The prince broke with Mrs Fitzherbert and suggested marriage with his cousin Princess

Caroline of Brunswick, though enquiries reported that among her defects was an unfortunate lack of interest in personal cleanliness. Pitt's proposal that the prince's income should be more than doubled to £121,000, a further £77,000 granted for wedding and domestic expenses, and the establishment of a sinking fund to repay his debt within twenty-seven years, was badly received. There was a rebellion of several of the government's most trusted supporters, and Pitt was obliged to inform the king that it could not be carried. Meanwhile the opposition hinted that the king himself could be more generous. The amount set aside for the redemption of debt had to be increased. The marriage, which took place on 8 April 1795, was in all other respects an unmitigated disaster, though Princess Charlotte was conceived on what was said to be the first and last nuptial night, and born on 7 January 1796. Three days later the prince made a will leaving all his property (largely debt) to Maria Fitzherbert, 'my wife, the wife of my heart and soul' (*Correspondence of George, Prince of Wales*, 3.133, no. 1067). In February the prince was forced to beg the king to prevent bailiffs moving into Carlton House, and in March he announced his intention of separating from the princess. To compound matters, Queen Charlotte wrote to the king on 15 April 1796 that she could no longer pay her tradesmen.

Ireland and the breach with Pitt

Meanwhile war against revolutionary France raged. The main political problem concerned Ireland. Strategically it was a point of weakness since a French landing might expect considerable Irish support, but Ireland was potentially a great source of recruitment to the British armed forces if the population was loyal. In 1782 the volunteers had done more to promote Irish interests than to frighten the enemy and Pitt was not anxious for a repetition. An early concession in 1793 was an Irish Act allowing Roman Catholics to vote, to hold certain restricted and defined public appointments, and to attend Trinity College, Dublin. Since legislative independence had been granted in 1782 it did not need British ratification, though Pitt's cabinet was in full support. There is no evidence that George III opposed the concession—indeed he gave a courteous welcome to a Catholic committee deputation and the Catholics in turn voted £2000 for a statue of the king in Dublin—but the measure was certain to raise expectations of full emancipation: the right to sit in parliament. On that question the king certainly had an opinion.

The issue touched on in 1793 exploded in 1795. Westmorland, the lord lieutenant, had been appalled at the British government's concessions and had carried them in the Irish parliament with great reluctance. He was recalled in 1795 and his successor, Lord Fitzwilliam, one of the Portland whigs, primed by Burke, undertook an abrupt reversal of policy, favouring Catholic emancipation and dismissing many of the office-holders, who appealed to Pitt for redress. The ensuing crisis nearly wrecked the newly formed coalition. Fitzwilliam's headstrong conduct raised undue expectations, Pitt was not prepared to abandon responsibility in so important an area, and when George III belatedly learned what was intended he was horrified. He protested his 'greatest astonishment' at the 'total change of the principles of government, which have been followed by every administration in that kingdom since the abdication of King James the Second' (Stanhope, 2.appx, xxiii). He pointed out that his family had been invited to the throne specifically to protect the protestant state, and warned that the subject was beyond the authority of the cabinet to determine without wider consultation. There was no confrontation, however, between the monarch and the cabinet because Fitzwilliam's colleagues also concluded that he had badly overplayed his hand. They resolved on Fitzwilliam's recall after only seven weeks in Dublin.

Irish affairs dominated much of the remainder of George III's active political life, against the background of the war against revolutionary and then Napoleonic France. After 1795 discontent in Ireland increased, demonstrating to the conservatives that the Irish were incorrigibly disloyal, and to the liberals that the reforms had been inadequate. Pitt had for some time considered that a union of Ireland with Britain might be desirable; after the great rebellion of 1798, which had been belatedly assisted by French troops, the case seemed overwhelming. Catholic emancipation could then be granted for the Westminster parliament in the knowledge that Catholic MPs in a United Kingdom would remain a small minority. With the general principle of union the king was in agreement. It came into effect on 1 January 1801, with George proclaimed king of the United Kingdom of Great Britain and Ireland. The old claim to be king of France was at last abandoned. George had been asked whether he wished to be known as 'Emperor of the British Isles', but replied that he was satisfied with the title of king (*Later Correspondence of George III*, 3.435n., no. 2274).

But if the king had been hostile to Catholic emancipation in Ireland in 1795, he was unshakeably opposed to it for Britain as a whole, regarding it as a breach of his coronation oath. In January 1799 he had warned Pitt that 'though a strong friend to the Union of the two kingdoms, I should become an enemy to the measure if I thought a change in the situation of the Roman Catholics would attend this measure' (*Later Correspondence of George III*, 3.186 n. 2, no. 1914). Pitt, harassed and unwell, neglected to inform George what the cabinet was contemplating, leaving others to draw it to his notice. It was a subject on which George felt most strongly. On 28 January 1801, at his levee, he approached Henry Dundas 'in a loud voice and agitated manner', asked him what was going on, and declared that he would regard as his personal enemy any man who proposed Catholic emancipation to him (Ehrman, 3.503). Pitt called a cabinet at once, postponed the opening of parliament, and wrote to the king that his own opinion in favour of emancipation was 'unalterably fixed'. George replied that his coronation oath did not allow him to consent to a measure 'no less than the complete overthrow of the whole fabric' of the constitution in church and state, but if Pitt agreed not to urge the proposal, the king would keep his opinions to himself (Stanhope, 3.appx, xxvi, xxix). He then approached Henry Addington, speaker of the House of Commons and a friend of Pitt, to form a new administration. The whole crisis was over in a week. No one could argue that Pitt had not had fair warning or that it was not a matter so close to the prerogative and status of the monarchy that the king had a right to be consulted. The tactic of using the king's name against his ministers was a startling repetition of the events of December 1783 which had overthrown the Fox–North coalition and brought Pitt to power, yet Pitt and the king parted with great regret and expressions of mutual esteem.

Decline and oblivion

The failure of an experimental peace

It is not easy to know whether the next and ominous development was a cause or a consequence of the political upheaval. But on 13 February 1801, amid the crisis, the king was unwell, and by the 17th he was excited, talkative, and hoarse. On the 21st he told Thomas Willis, son of Francis Willis and rector of St George's, Bloomsbury, 'I have prayed to God all night, that I might die, or that he would spare my reason' (Brooke, *King George the Third*, 370). That night he became delirious, and the next day John Willis, Thomas's brother and a now a mad-doctor like their father, was called in to take charge of the king; he was subsequently joined by a third Willis brother, Robert. This bout of illness formally lasted some four weeks, officially ending by 14 March when the king was well enough to receive the seals of office from Pitt, and thereby avoiding putting into effect plans for a regency. It took longer for the king to extricate himself from his doctors, as he continued to show signs of agitation for several months; on 19 April he was effectively kidnapped by the Willises, with the queen's support, and was not able to escape them until 19 May. His illness left George thinner, exhausted, and less resilient, and his eyesight was also causing concern. Worst of all, under the severe strain his relations with the queen had deteriorated. She was terrified of a return of violence and perhaps upset by his obscene language in delirium. The queen was a firm supporter of the Willises, whose methods the king detested. Her temper worsened, much of it directed at the princesses, and she locked her bedroom door against her husband. 'It is a melancholy circumstance', remarked Lord Hobart, 'to see a family that had lived so well together, for such a number of years, completely broken up' (*Journal and Correspondence of…Auckland*, 4.214).

Pitt made a formal pledge to the king that he would not again raise the question of Catholic emancipation, and at first gave strong support to his successor, Henry Addington. The king agreed to peace negotiations being opened, though he had never thought that any understanding with republican France was likely, and he described the treaty of Amiens, signed in 1802, as an 'experimental peace'. The experiment failed, and the renewal of the war in May 1803 made the recall of Pitt only a matter of time. The country braced itself for a Napoleonic invasion, and the king wrote to Bishop Hurd in November 1803 in heroic terms: 'should his troops effect a landing, I shall certainly put myself at the head of mine...to repel them' (Jesse, 3.330). It was not very practical but entirely in character. But early in the new year there were signs of a recurrence of his illness, with continuous talking and hurry. Addington sent for the Willises, but the dukes of Kent and Cumberland refused them access. Dr Samuel Simmons replaced them, but the strait-jacket was still employed. The severe attack lasted only a week, but recovery was protracted and intermittent. George was at once confronted with another political crisis arising from the negotiations for Pitt's return. The king parted from Addington with great reluctance, wishing to reward 'the best friend he has in the world' (Ziegler, 222–3) with an earldom and pension. At an audience on 7 May 1804 Pitt found the king remarkably composed and in total command of the situation. Pitt repeated his promise not to raise the Catholic question. The king had already vetoed the inclusion of Charles James Fox, though suggesting, perhaps sardonically, that he might be offered an ambassadorship. Grenville refused to serve without Fox, and Pitt's hope for 'a strong and comprehensive government, uniting the principal weight and talents of public men of all descriptions' (Stanhope, 4.appx, xii) to deal with the French menace did not materialize.

Pitt's second ministry survived until his death in January 1806. It was fraught with difficulties. The third coalition against France was destroyed by Napoleon's victories at Ulm and Austerlitz, though Nelson's triumph at Trafalgar in October 1805 removed the last threat of a French invasion. The king's position was very odd. He was no longer under restraint after February 1804 but was easily disturbed and in need of constant attention. On 16 May 1804 his new prime minister and Lord Chancellor Eldon wrote to beg him, on medical advice, 'to avoid too frequent or protracted audiences and conversations' (Stanhope, 4.appx, xv). In December 1804 he expressed his joy that Pitt and Addington were reconciled, and Addington joined the government in January 1805 as lord president of the council. But the disgrace and impeachment of Henry Dundas, now Viscount Melville, long one of Pitt's closest friends, caused the prime minister great distress, and led to Addington's resigning once more. Grenville and Fox, in opposition, were short of numbers, but watchful and persistent. In May 1805 they moved to exploit the Catholic difficulty by proposing a committee on the subject. To the king's satisfaction they were defeated in the Lords by 178 votes to 49, and in the Commons by 336 votes to 124. George's attitude towards Pitt remained friendly, but he was increasingly unpredictable, particularly over court appointments, and Pitt's awareness that a regency would probably mean his own dismissal, curbed his powers of remonstrance. In January 1805 there was a very sharp quarrel, with raised voices, over the vacant archbishopric of Canterbury. The king carried his candidate, Manners-Sutton, against Pitt's former tutor Tomline, even though Pitt hinted at resignation and warned the king how much it must weaken his position. But the king's precarious state of health meant that the situation was quite abnormal and, paradoxically, gave him a temporary advantage.

Moreover, in the light of so many discussions on the relationship of church and state, arising from the Catholic issue, the king was certain to be sensitive on ecclesiastical matters, and regarded the appointment as well within the remit of his royal authority.

Politics after Pitt

William Pitt's death on 23 January 1806 opened the way for the 'ministry of all the talents' which he had failed to construct in 1804. The king had little choice of prime minister. The cabinet met immediately and decided that it could not form the basis for a new administration and that resort to the opposition must be had. Addington had clearly demonstrated that he was not the man to lead a great national struggle for survival, though the king was reported to have approached him and also to have sounded out Lord Hawkesbury. George sent for Lord Grenville, knowing that this would mean accepting Fox as a minister, though he had once declared that he would rather risk civil war. Addington was brought back as lord privy seal while the rest of the Pittites moved into opposition. At the inescapable audience with Fox, who took the ministry for foreign affairs, the king was composed and conciliatory: 'Mr Fox, I little thought you and I should ever meet again in this place. But I have no desire to look back upon old grievances, and you may rest assured I shall never remind you of them' (Jesse, 3.474). He found Fox's manner perfectly acceptable though, in the event, he did not have to accept it for long: by June 1806 Fox was gravely ill and he died in September. His hopes of peace with Napoleon had gone, but his other great objective—abolition of the slave trade, about which the king was unenthusiastic—was in good shape. Fox was replaced by Lord Howick, the future prime minister Earl Grey.

The issue of Catholic emancipation was avoided at the foundation of the 'ministry of all the talents', but the Irish Catholics had no reason to be equally circumspect, and in January 1807, much to the irritation of Grenville and his colleagues, they prepared to submit a petition. This threatened both the unity of the cabinet, where Sidmouth was strongly opposed to concessions, and its relations with the monarch. The duke of Bedford, lord lieutenant of Ireland, suggested that some small concessions might persuade the Catholic committee to hold its fire. Grenville's original intention was merely to extend the 1793 Irish

Act to Britain, thus taking account of the union, and allowing British Catholics to hold commissions up to staff rank. It would have the additional advantage of encouraging recruitment at a time of manpower shortage. The cabinet was well aware that it would not be easy to persuade the king to accept even this modest concession, but after protest he did so, Grenville writing to Dublin Castle that royal approval had been obtained with difficulty, but 'with proofs of temper and good will...Beyond this, I am perfectly satisfied he will not go' (*Fortescue MSS*, 9.37). But Bedford, Elliot, and Buckingham warned him that so slight a concession would do nothing to buy off the Irish Catholics. Indeed, there was no reason why it should, since it benefited only British Catholics and protestant dissenters. The government therefore changed the terms, agreeing that the concession must apply to all ranks, including staff appointments—which the 1793 act had not. The day before the revised measure was due to be presented to parliament by Howick, the king complained that the concessions were far greater than he had been led to believe and threatened to use his veto if the bill passed. Grenville agreed to withdraw the measure on the condition that his cabinet reserved the right to express their opinions on the Catholic question. George III refused to concede this and looked for an alternative administration. Portland then formed his second ministry out of the remnants of the Pitt survivors, with Spencer Perceval as leader in the Commons.

Recriminations and accusations of bad faith abounded, and the episode went down in whig legend as a stab in the back by the crown. The crisis blew up quickly out of Irish affairs, the king and ministers had many other matters to consider, and the legislation was rushed. Howick admitted rather lamely that he had 'not sufficiently attended to the distinction between it and the Irish Act' (*Hansard 1*, 9, 1807, 267–8). But the fact that the legislation had started life as a mere amendment to the Mutiny Bill and was then brought forward as a bill in its own right indicates a significant shift in the ministers' position. They had already been warned, in unmistakable terms, that the original concession was as far as the king would go, and they decided to attempt to slide the change past George III. The most careful and scholarly study of the episode concluded that the whigs were engaged in 'a sort of juggle' (Roberts, 32), which the king saw through. Two later studies, the biographies of Lord Grey by John Derry and E. A. Smith, concurred—the ministers attempted to 'smuggle' (Roberts, 22) the extended bill past the king. Fortunately for the whigs their dismissal enabled them to present themselves as deeply injured men, martyred in the cause of toleration and progress.

Darkness

With the advent of Portland's government, George III's political problems were almost at an end, though the outcome of the war remained in the balance and the Spanish campaign caused great anxiety in 1808 and 1809. Portland's conservative anti-Catholic ministry was close to the king's own views and one of its first moves was to obtain a dissolution (the second within eight months) and win a handsome victory at the general election. Portland was in bad health when he took office—'I have often been with him when I thought he would have died in his chair', wrote Malmesbury—but he survived until the autumn of 1809 (*Diaries and Correspondence*, 4.413). His successor, Spencer Perceval, steady, experienced, and a staunch Anglican, was entirely acceptable to George, and he saw out the king's effective reign.

George's family difficulties did not diminish. The continuing rift between the prince and princess of Wales caused acute embarrassment, and the rumours that the princess had had an illegitimate son led to the establishment of the 'delicate investigation' of 1806. Though the report declared that there was 'no foundation whatever' for the allegation, it added that the princess's conduct had been such as to encourage 'very unfavourable interpretations' (*Correspondence of George, Prince of Wales*, 5.403–4, no. 2196). The king was less critical of the princess than some of his family, but recriminations rumbled on, with Caroline asking for accommodation in Carlton House and for assistance with her mounting debts. In 1809 Colonel Wardle's accusation in the House of Commons that the duke of York, the king's favourite son and commander-in-chief, was guilty of corruption in selling commissions through his mistress, Mary Anne Clarke, forced the duke's resignation in March. At the same time there was growing concern over the health of the king's youngest and favourite daughter, Princess Amelia, who spent two months at Weymouth in the autumn of 1809 in search of recovery. The arrangements for the king's jubilee—the entrance to his fiftieth year on the throne, on 25 October 1809—though the occasion for widespread popular celebrations, were overshadowed for the royal family by these personal misfortunes. On 31 May 1810, another son, the duke of Cumberland, was found covered in blood, with his valet, Sellis, dead in a nearby room. The jury found that Sellis had attacked the duke and then committed suicide, but insinuations circulated that the duke himself had been the aggressor. By the summer of 1810 it was apparent that Princess Amelia was dying.

The last public appearance of the king was at a reception at Windsor on 25 October 1810, the anniversary of his succession. He appeared flustered and excited. Within days his former symptoms had returned and recourse was had to the strait-jacket. Princess Amelia died on 2 November 1810 and, following an act of parliament, a regency was declared on 7 February 1811. The Regency Act entrusted the care of the king's person to the queen, advised by a council of seven privy councillors headed by the archbishop of Canterbury. The council was to receive daily reports from the king's physicians and to send them a questionnaire

on the king's symptoms and chances of recovery
every three months.

Many people this time expected a fairly speedy recovery, attributing the king's illness to concern for his daughter. But though at first there were lucid intervals his condition worsened, and the last ten years of his life were spent in a twilight world. His eyesight deteriorated until he was completely blind and he was increasingly afflicted by deafness. Treatment was left in the hands of the mad-doctors, John and Robert Willis and Samuel Simmons, with the queen's blessing, and for the most part conventional physicians were excluded from day-to-day access to the king. Deprived for the most part of the stimulus of visitors, conversation, and outings, he took refuge in the past, sometimes real, often invented, talking to Lord North, long dead, and inspecting imaginary parades. 'In short' wrote Dr Heberden, 'he appears to be living in another world and has lost almost all interest in the concerns of this' (Macalpine and Hunter, 160–61). On 12 October 1814 George was declared king of Hanover at the Congress of Vienna, his German territories having been recovered earlier in the year after a decade in other hands. He was, however, never aware of this promotion. Following the queen's death in 1818 the duke of York took over formal responsibilities towards the king's health, but this brought no change in the medical regime. Towards the end he was a detached observer of his own misfortunes. One of his remaining pleasures was to play the harpsichord which had once belonged to Handel, hammering at the keyboard in an effort to hear; to his attendant he confided that it was a favourite piece of the late king, when he was alive. He died at Windsor on 29 January 1820, and was buried in St George's Chapel, Windsor, on the evening of 15 February.

The legacy and reputation of George III

Cultural bequests

George III had an important influence on national cultural life. On ascending the throne he determined to add to the library given by his royal predecessors to the British Museum. In the course of his reign he assembled 'one of the finest libraries ever created by one man' (Miller, 125). He was advised in this process by his librarian, Sir Frederick Barnard, and by Samuel Johnson, among others; by the time of his death it consisted of 65,250 volumes, 19,000 tracts and pamphlets, and the first large British collection of maps and charts. The king was also interested in typography and the design of books, establishing a royal bindery at Buckingham House. The royal collection was organized in three or more series, stored chiefly at Windsor and Buckingham House.

After George III's death his son George IV offered the library to the nation, and after protracted and complex negotiations it entered the British Museum, becoming known as the King's Library and acting as a valuable stimulus to the extension of the museum in the form of 'a proper building for the reception of the Royal Library' (Miller, 128). For a century and a half the King's Library was the oldest and most elegant part of the British Museum. It now forms the visual centre of the British Library at St Pancras.

The king was also an important art collector, as well as being a competent architectural draughtsman. His accession was 'a watershed in the history of the royal collection' (Millar, xi). In 1762 he bought the large collection of Joseph Smith, British consul in Venice, to put into Buckingham House, which he had just acquired. He commissioned portraits and other works of art from a number of contemporary artists, including a series of portraits of the royal family from Thomas Gainsborough, and he played an important part in the establishment of the Royal Academy in 1768, providing it with accommodation and with some initial funding, though he became notorious for his interference in appointments and art patronage. George III's state portrait was by Allan Ramsay (1761–2), with the king full length, in his coronation robes, and an accompanying portrait of the queen in hers. Ramsay also provided the king's profile for the new coinage. In 1781 Gainsborough painted a further and much admired full-length pair of the king and queen, the king's being regarded by Horace Walpole as 'very like, but stiff and raw' (Millar, xx). George III commissioned portraits of the queen and various members of his family from Sir Thomas Lawrence, but not one of himself.

The formal image of George III was made available to the public through engravings of the portraits by Ramsay and Gainsborough and other artists; but possibly more memorable were the uses to which caricaturists put George's features. James Gillray developed a distinct characterization for his George III: increasingly rotund as the 1780s and 1790s progressed, the king was depicted as frugal to the point of avarice, grasping money-bags with the queen in 'Vices overlook'd in the new proclamation' (24 May 1792, National Portrait Gallery, London, D12456) and devoted to his egg-cup in 'Temperance enjoying a frugal meal' (28 July 1792, NPG D12461) but also as a John

Bull, the embodiment of British and domestic virtues, and possessing an innocence in his royal status, whether as a potential assassination target surprised on the close-stool with the news of the murder of Gustav III of Sweden in 'Taking physick' (11 April 1792, NPG D13010) or well-meaningly terrorizing a tenant farmer in 'Affability' (10 February 1795, NPG D12518). The king was the focus of ridicule, but was often portrayed more affectionately than other targets of the satirical printmakers.

George III and the historians

It is not immediately apparent why George III became one of the most controversial and criticized monarchs in British history. Liberals disliked his hostility to parliamentary reform and Catholic emancipation; Americans condemned him as an oppressor of their country. There is little in this. Monarchs are not often found in the vanguard of reform and those who are, like Joseph II of Austria, were not conspicuously successful. The Americans' quarrel was with parliament, though they skilfully dramatized and personalized it by blaming the king. One reason for such widespread condemnation is that many of the early printed sources, greatly used by nineteenth-century historians, were hostile to George III. Much of the historical writing of the twentieth century was devoted to scraping away accumulated layers of myth and distortion. Edmund Burke's *Thoughts on the Cause of the Present Discontents* (1770) popularized the idea that George governed through a double cabinet—a set of secret advisers—though there is scant evidence to support it and the theory was little more than an attempt to excuse the Rockinghams' remarkable lack of success. Not only would such a system have been extremely difficult to operate in a small political circle, in which all major politicians were watched, but it would have sat oddly with the constant changes in the official and avowed personnel. Horace Walpole, whose *Memoirs of the Reign of King George the Third* were first published in 1845, wove a gothick romance around an attempt by the king, encouraged by his scheming mother and her paramour Lord Bute, to achieve prerogative and absolute power. Lord John Russell, an apostolic whig, whose edition of the correspondence of the duke of Bedford came out in 1846, insisted that 'the project of restoring to the crown that absolute direction and control which Charles I and James II had been forced to relinquish ... was entertained and attempted by George III' (*Correspondence of...Bedford*, 3.xxix). For this there is no evidence at all. One of George's earliest schoolroom essays praised the revolution of 1688 as the foundation of British religion and liberty, and for saving the country from arbitrary power. If George III had any desire to increase the power of the crown, it was within the context of the revolution settlement, not against it. Despite the fact that J. W. Croker, in his brilliant review of Walpole's *Memoirs*, warned against 'pertinacious attempts to poison history', the hostile interpretation of George continued to hold the field (J. W. Croker, 'Review of *Memoirs of the Reign of King George III* by Horace Walpole', *Quarterly Review*, 77, 1845–6, 274). Sir George Otto Trevelyan declared in 1880 that the king 'invariably declared himself upon the wrong side in a controversy' (Trevelyan, 122), and W. E. H. Lecky in 1882 wrote of George that 'it may be said without exaggeration that he inflicted more profound and enduring injuries upon his country than any other modern English king' (Lecky, 3.14). As late as 1937 this view was expressed, in its crudest form, in a review of C. E. Vulliamy's *Royal George*, which suggested that the king made 'the last attempt to foist a dictatorship on Britain' (Barnes, vii).

Magisterial judgements went out of fashion in the mainstream of twentieth-century historiography. In his Oxford Ford lectures for 1934 L. B. Namier began the process of reassessment, arguing that in 1760 the king's right to choose his own ministers was not a provocation but a commonplace. Romney Sedgwick, in his edition of George III's letters to Lord Bute of 1939, denied G. M. Trevelyan's contention that there was a break in 'the smooth development of our constitutional history in 1760', and attributed any enhanced influence of the crown after 1760 to the fact that for twenty years there was no rival reversionary interest (Sedgwick, introduction, *Letters … to Lord Bute*, xvi). Richard Pares, in the Ford lectures for 1951, took an intermediate position: there was no fundamental difference in the situations of George II and George III, but the latter's more conscientious personality meant 'a more active royalty' (Pares, 61–2). Namier had a chance to restate his own position in 1953 with his Academy of Arts lecture, 'King George III: a study of personality', concluding that 'in reality the constitutional practice of George III differed little from that of George I and George II', and calling him a 'much maligned ruler' (Namier, *Personalities and Powers*, 43, 58). J. B. Owen, attacking the problem from the other end in 'George II reconsidered', denied that George II was a weak or ineffective ruler, and maintained that the theory of the pivotal importance of 1760 was 'an accident of historiography' (Whiteman, 118).

Yet though to explode myths is an important part of the historian's task, it is not the only one, and something must be put in their place. In his critique of Namier, Herbert Butterfield remarked that he and his associates came close to denying George III any views at all. Several of the king's ambitions were clear, and not necessarily contentious. His desire to discourage vice and to set an example of duty and respectability was welcomed by many of his subjects, particularly in the middle class of society. His aspiration to eradicate party was highly predictable. It was the ambition of most monarchs, attracted by the concept of national unity, as well as the increased flexibility which a non-party approach offered; many of George's contemporaries were still profoundly ambivalent towards party, regarding it as self-seeking and factious. His wish to eliminate corruption may have been pious and ill-defined—a mere parrot phrase of the patriot opposition of the 1730s—but such ideas can strike root, and the elimination of pensions and sinecures was to become a very popular programme in the later eighteenth century. In this instance, liberal historians failed to identify George as 'on the right side'.

A king in context

An important explanation of George's difficulties is that the revolution settlement of 1688, which he admired so greatly, while establishing the broad framework for limited monarchy, left many everyday questions unresolved. There was ambiguity at the heart of the eighteenth-century system, even if commentators dignified it as balance. The practical working of the constitution was being decided in the politics of the period, not in theoretical discussions or in legislation, but in the daily struggles for power. In a reign of fifty active years, in so fluid a situation, almost all of the undecided issues of the revolution settlement came into discussion, and produced sharp confrontations.

The precise powers of the crown were far from clear. The formal limitations which the revolution settlement, reinforced by the Act of Settlement, imposed on monarchs were important, but few. They could not be Catholics nor marry a Catholic. They could not use the suspending power, or the dispensing power as it had been used of late. They could not dismiss judges, nor maintain an army in peacetime without parliamentary approval. To that extent the door had been bolted against popery and autocracy. What they positively could do was not spelled out. The veto was not employed after Anne's reign, but nobody could say whether it had become obsolete, and its use was considered in 1783 and again in 1807. It was agreed that the monarch must choose ministers, but the effective use of this prerogative depended upon alternative men being available. This was not the case in March 1783 or January 1806, but was in January 1770 and December 1783. Peers had an undisputed right to private audience and to offer advice, but this sat awkwardly with the theory of responsible ministers. The acceptance of the propriety of opposition—perhaps the key element in the idea of parliamentary government—was a plant of slow growth in the eighteenth century, tainted by treason as long as an active Jacobite cause survived, but remaining something that many men were uneasy with for decades after the battle of Culloden. By position and temperament

George III found opposition peculiarly hard to
come to terms with: 'I have no wish but for the
prosperity of my dominions', he wrote angrily
in November 1782, 'therefore must look on all
who will not heartily assist me as bad men as
well as ungrateful subjects' (*Correspondence*, ed.
Fortescue, 6.151, no. 3973). The lord chancellor
retained a special position as the king's man in
the cabinet and the keeper of the royal conscience,
yet when he clashed with the first minister, as
Thurlow did with Pitt in 1792, he was forced out.
The office of first minister was developing, from
an unpleasant term of abuse directed at Sir Robert
Walpole, through characteristic evasion by North,
to an avowed and formal exposition of its necessity by William Pitt in 1803. It was a development which militated strongly against the powers
remaining to the monarch. Parliamentary government evolved as a means of resolving conflict
peacefully, and to that extent disagreement was
built into the system, but the nineteenth-century
method of finally deciding such matters by means
of a general election had not yet come about.
The king chose and dismissed ministers, and it
was therefore inescapable that what he decided
could be greatly resented. The constitution which
George III admired so much avoided civil war

and *coups d'état*, but it functioned with creaks and groans.

It is scarcely surprising that George III found, at times, so delicate and shifting a position difficult to understand and to operate. It called for much compromise, conciliation, and tact. Patronage and honours questions—another grey area between the monarch and his ministers—provided a never-ending source of discontent and irritation, to say nothing of more profound issues of war and peace. In the middle of the American crisis George declared that he would take refuge in his closet and see no one, not because of military disasters, but because he could not face quarrels about peerage promotions.

Yet it would be both unprofitable and misleading to attempt to trace the many difficulties to which these ambiguities gave rise in a long reign, since it would mean an undue concentration on the malfunctioning of the constitution. But four episodes in which the king's conduct was much criticized may briefly be mentioned. The elevation of Lord Bute in 1760 was clearly an error of judgement. But it was neither unconstitutional nor unusual. Monarchs usually brought their friends forward at the outset of their reigns. Anne had elevated the Marlboroughs on her 'sunshine day'; George I had dismissed the tories and called in the whigs; George II intended to promote his favourite Sir Spencer Compton, and it had been the intention of Frederick, prince of Wales, to place power in the hands of Lord Egmont. Indeed, George III insisted upon Bute's taking office to counter any complaint that he was a minister behind the curtain. It should be remembered that Bute was supported in parliament by large majorities and, despite inexperience, his performance in the House of Lords was far from foolish—certainly compared with that of Lord Rockingham. The other three episodes, in 1783, 1801, and 1807, were superficially similar in character, involving accusations that the king had deliberately deceived his ministers. But in practice they were very different. The king's intervention against the Fox–North coalition in December 1783 does not seem to have been preceded by any warning to Portland that he disapproved of the India Bill, nor was the use of the king's name easy to reconcile, as Fitzwilliam and North argued, with responsible government. The extraordinary nature of the king's action is confirmed by the fact that nobody tried to defend it: Pitt, who had insisted on it as a *sine qua non* before taking office, pretended that the rumours were 'the lie of the day' (Cobbett, *Parliamentary History*, 24, 1783, 202). George's reply would have been that so unnatural a coalition, depriving him of any choice of ministers, was tantamount to a breach or breakdown of the constitution, and justified him in using the means he did to free himself; they were not his ministers but men who had forced themselves on him. His belief was endorsed by national opinion at the election of 1784.

Pitt's resignation in 1801 was quite different. The king had no wish to part with his minister and did so with sincere expressions of regret and esteem. His outburst to Dundas at the levee seems to have been unpremeditated, the result of his conscientious scruples over his coronation oath. It would be hard to argue that the monarch of a dynasty brought in specifically and only because it was protestant should not have the right to object to concessions to the Catholics. Nor can one deny that there was a plausible case for George's belief that concessions to the Catholic Irish, far from bringing reconciliation and loyalty, would merely promote fresh demands and pave the way for independence. In the third example, of 1807, the evidence suggests strongly that the proposed legislation had not been adequately explained to the king, that he had given a very deliberate warning of his disapproval, but that he used the occasion to part with a ministry which he had accepted with reluctance and now mistrusted.

George III and the popular imagination

George III's perceived failings as a king, politician, and man, inspired much ink pouring by historians and essayists, but he made little impact on literature. His cameo appearance in Thackeray's *Barry Lyndon* (1844) was as the cold or weak head of a hypocritical social elite. In the twentieth century occasional cinema portrayals left no time for any development of the king's place in the popular historical memory: Robert Morley's depiction in *Beau Brummell* (1954) was of a wide-eyed monarch on the fringes of insanity. By the late 1980s it seemed that the king was becoming confused with his grandfather and great-grandfather: the BBC television comedy series *Blackadder the Third* (1987) introduced at its climax a German-accented George III, obsessed with sausages and penguins and wearing a tree branch in his hair, presumably a nod to the discredited story that the king had once mistaken an oak tree in Windsor Great Park for the king of Prussia.

George III was rescued from such ignominy by Alan Bennett's play *The Madness of George III*, first performed in 1991 at the Royal National Theatre, London. Bennett's picture of the king's historical reputation was derived from his reading of Herbert Butterfield and Richard Pares in the 1950s, through a knowledge that subsequent writers such as Brooke, Macalpine and Hunter had made him 'No longer the ogre... altogether more kindly, wiser even' (A. Bennett, *The Madness of George III*, 1992, viii) and that the saga of his treatment by doctors, incomprehending of his condition, would make him a tragic hero to the audience. Bennett acknowledged that Nigel Hawthorne, who originated the part of the king, transformed the role, and newspaper critics who had reservations about the play itself endorsed Hawthorne's performance—'to order, vulgar, witty, pompous, humble, pathetic, raving, razor-sharp' (*The Independent*, 30 November 1991). Hawthorne and the play's director, Nicholas Hytner, transferred with Bennett to the rewritten cinema version, *The Madness of King George* (1994). The film took more liberties with the historical account than had the stage play, but strengthened the sympathetic depiction of a conscientious man always acutely aware of his responsibility and status, until illness stripped that away. If George III has ceased to be a cipher in the popular imagination, and instead is remembered as a human being, Hawthorne, Bennett, and Hytner have some claim to the credit.

Character and achievement

One charge repeatedly made against George III— and strangely at odds with his popular image as a plain, honest gentleman—was that of duplicity. It was a favourite accusation of Wilkes and Junius, and erected by Horace Walpole into a 'habit of dissimulation' (Walpole, *Memoirs*, 1.16). But none of them (assuming that Sir Philip Francis *was* Junius) knew the king well enough to make his opinion of much value, and these remarks may be dismissed as general political abuse. Chatham, after his comeback in 1770, complained that he had been undermined by secret influence, and Shelburne, briefly a royal favourite in 1782, believed afterwards that he had been betrayed by the king, of whom he spoke bitterly as a man who 'obtained your confidence, procured from you your opinion of different public characters, and then availed himself of this knowledge to sow dissension' (J. Nicholls, *Recollections and Reflections, Personal and Political, as Connected with Public Affairs, during the Reign of George III,* 1820, 1822, 1.389). There was little need for the king to sow dissension in the Chatham or Shelburne ministries—it grew of its own accord. But although George had done his best to sustain and encourage each of them, it suited them to suspect treachery and cry 'foul'.

The reality is rather the reverse. Far from being a master of dissimulation the king, a man of strong feelings and with an excitable nature, found it hard to dissemble, and might have had an easier life had he cared less deeply about his duty and been more willing to give way with good grace. Namier, ruminating on a lifetime devoted to George's early reign, concluded: 'what I have never been able to find is the man arrogating power to himself, the ambitious schemer out to dominate, the intriguer dealing in an underhand fashion with his Ministers' (Namier, *Personalities and Powers*, 57). But another explanation of the charge was the ambiguity of George's position as both head of society and active politician.

Most monarchs develop defences against impor-
tunity: Charles II is said to have walked very
fast, while George II's temper was enough to
keep most petitioners at bay. George III found
the stylized routine of court life rather difficult, and his famously repeated interjections—
'What? What?' (for example, *Diary and Letters of
Madame D'Arblay*, 14 December 1785, 2.275)—
were attempts to fill awkward gaps and silences.
He replaced his initial shyness by bland and vague
assurances, which others sometimes mistook, or
pretended to mistake, for promises. His conservative attitude and liking for a routine life made
him prefer ministers whom he knew and was
comfortable with, and if he subsequently turned
against them, it was not that he was ruthless
and unfeeling, but that often the ministers, like
Chatham, North, Shelburne, and Pitt, had drifted
into opposition. George III, like many men in
public life, found it hard to distinguish political
from personal friendship and, as a result, often felt
betrayed. Even Bute had, in the end, disappointed
him.

The reign of George III saw a long and unspectac-
ular decline in the power of the monarchy. This
was to some extent masked from contemporaries

by the difficulty they experienced in distinguishing between the crown and the government in a period in which the two were so closely related. Dunning's motion of 1780—'that the influence of the crown has increased, is increasing, and ought to be diminished'—was a political slogan not an impartial analysis, and a commentary on the government rather than on the monarchy's share in it. The causes of the crown's decline were many and insidious, but included the great growth in public opinion (manifested in newspapers and petitions), the consolidation of party loyalties which ultimately diminished the crown's choice of ministers, the financial debility of the monarchy, the decline in crown patronage, the rise in the power of the first minister, and the growing complexity of public business—the last of which also sounded the knell for the amateur gentleman in politics. George III fought a steady and not unsuccessful rearguard action for the rights of the monarchy, conscious of his duty, determined to remain briefed and informed, but increasingly handicapped by age and ill health. As he must have suspected, his son had neither the stamina nor the character to preserve the position his father handed on to him in 1810. In the course of George III's reign the monarch had been

increasingly forced on to the defensive; he could
object, frustrate, delay, and obstruct, but he no
longer had much power of initiative. He could
keep Charles James Fox out, but he could not
keep Bute, Grafton, North, and Addington in. His
two most controversial actions were, significantly,
negative ones—against the India Bill and against
Catholic emancipation. In each case he was supported by the voters, at the general elections of
1784 and 1807. But in the event of hostile public
opinion the king would have been dangerously
exposed.

In some respects George's reign was a dress
rehearsal for the even longer reign of his grand-
daughter, Queen Victoria. Probably unwittingly,
George had shown the way out of the ambiguities
of the monarch's role, moving to a position less
prominent politically, and substituting a concept
of the monarchy as the symbol of the nation, a
pattern of duty and respectability—'the head of
our *morality*' in Walter Bagehot's phrase—which
Victoria, Albert, and their descendants were to
develop (*Collected Works*, 5.235). George was an
unlucky man whom life treated badly and whose
talents did not quite fit the situation in which he
found himself. But he cannot be faulted for want

of effort. 'I do not pretend to any superior abilities', he wrote, 'but will give place to no one in meaning to preserve the freedom, happiness and glory of my dominions and all their inhabitants, and to fulfill the duty to my God and my neighbour in the most extended sense' (J. Brooke, frontispiece, *King George the Third*, new edn, 1985).

Sources

The correspondence of King George the Third from 1760 to December 1783, ed. J. Fortescue, 6 vols. (1927–8) · *Letters from George III to Lord Bute, 1756–1766*, ed. R. Sedgwick (1939) · *The later correspondence of George III*, ed. A. Aspinall, 5 vols. (1962–70) · J. Brooke, *King George III* (1972) · S. Ayling, *George III* (1972) · H. Butterfield, *George III and the historians* (1957) · R. Pares, *George III and the politicians* (1955) · H. Walpole, *Memoirs of the reign of King George the Third*, ed. D. Le Marchant, 4 vols. (1845) · *The memoirs and speeches of James, 2nd Earl Waldegrave, 1742–1763*, ed. J. C. D. Clark (1988) · *The Yale edition of Horace Walpole's correspondence*, ed. W. S. Lewis and others, 48 vols. (1937–83) · J. H. Jesse, *Memoirs of the life and reign of King George the Third*, 2nd edn, 3 vols. (1867) · L. B. Namier, *Personalities and powers* (1955) · *The diary of the late George Bubb Dodington*, ed. W. P. Wyndham (1809) · *The diaries of a duchess: extracts from the diaries of the first duchess of Northumberland (1716–1776)*, ed. J. Greig (1926) · *Additional Grenville papers, 1763–1765*, ed. J. R. G. Tomlinson (1962) · *The Grenville papers: being the correspondence of Richard Grenville … and … George Grenville*, ed. W. J. Smith, 4 vols. (1852–3) · *Correspondence of John, fourth duke of Bedford*, ed. J. Russell, 3 vols. (1842–6) · *Memorials and correspondence of Charles James Fox*, ed. J. Russell, 4 vols. (1853–7) · Earl Stanhope [P. H. Stanhope], *Life of the Right Honourable William Pitt*, 4 vols. (1861–2) · Duke of Buckingham and Chandos [R. Grenville], *Memoirs of the court and cabinets of George the Third*, 4 vols. (1853–5) ·

H. R. Vassall, Lord Holland, *Memoirs of the whig party during my time*, ed. H. E. Vassall, Lord Holland, 2 vols. (1852–4) · *The Jenkinson papers, 1760–1766*, ed. N. S. Jucker (1949) · *Diary and letters of Madame D'Arblay*, ed. [C. Barrett], 7 vols. (1842–6) · *The correspondence of George, prince of Wales, 1770–1812*, ed. A. Aspinall, 8 vols. (1963–71) · D. G. Barnes, *George III and William Pitt, 1783–1806: a new interpretation based upon a study of their unpublished correspondence* (1939) · *The diaries and correspondence of the Right Hon. George Rose*, ed. L. V. V. Harcourt, 2 vols. (1860) · *The journal and correspondence of William, Lord Auckland*, ed. [G. Hogge], 4 vols. (1861–2) · *Diaries and correspondence of James Harris, first earl of Malmesbury*, ed. third earl of Malmesbury [J. H. Harris], 4 vols. (1844) · I. R. Christie, *Myth and reality in late-eighteenth-century British politics, and other papers* (1970) · J. W. Derry, *The regency crisis and the whigs, 1788–9* (1963) · P. Langford, *The first Rockingham administration, 1765–1766* (1973) · J. Cannon, *The Fox–North coalition: crisis of the constitution, 1782–4* (1969) · P. Ziegler, *Addington: a life of Henry Addington, first Viscount Sidmouth* (1965) · N. Gash, *Lord Liverpool* (1984) · I. Macalpine and R. Hunter, *George III and the mad-business* (1969) · M. Roberts, *The whig party, 1807–12* (1965) · *Autobiography and political correspondence of Augustus Henry, third duke of Grafton*, ed. W. R. Anson (1898) · J. W. Derry, *Charles, Earl Grey* (1992) · E. A. Smith, *Lord Grey, 1764–1845* (1990) · G. O. Trevelyan, *The early years of Charles James Fox* (1881) · L. Colley, 'The apotheosis of George III: loyalty, royalty, and the British nation, 1760–1820', *Past and Present*, 102 (1984), 94–129 · *The collected works of Walter Bagehot*, ed. N. St John-Stevas, 5 (1974) · W. E. H. Lecky, *A history of England in the eighteenth century*, 8 vols. (1879–90) · L. B. Namier, *Crossroads of power* (1962) · *A narrative of changes in the ministry, 1765–1767*, ed. M. Bateson, Camden Society, new ser., 59 (1898) · E. N. Williams, ed., *The eighteenth-century constitution, 1688–1815* (1960) · P. Mackesy, *The war for America, 1775–1783* (1964) · K. W. Schweizer, ed., *Lord Bute: essays in re-interpretation* (1988) · J. Brooke, *The Chatham administration, 1766–1768* (1956) · P. D. G. Thomas, *Lord North* (1976) · A. Whiteman, ed., *Statesmen, scholars and merchants: essays in eighteenth century history presented to Dame Lucy Sutherland* (1973) · J. Ehrman, *The younger Pitt*, 1: *The years of acclaim* (1969) · J. Ehrman, *The younger Pitt,*

2: *The reluctant transition* (1983) · J. Ehrman, *The younger Pitt*, 3: *The consuming struggle* (1996) · *The manuscripts of the marquess of Abergavenny, Lord Braye, G. F. Luttrell*, Historical Manuscripts Commission (HMC), 15 (1887) · *Eighth report*, 2, HMC, 7 (1910) · *The manuscripts of the earl of Lonsdale*, HMC, 33 (1893) · *The manuscripts of J. B. Fortescue*, 10 vols., HMC, 30 (1892–1927) · L. Namier and J. Brooke, eds., *The history of parliament: the House of Commons, 1754–1790*, 3 vols. (1964); repr. (1985) · R. G. Thorne, ed., *The history of parliament: the House of Commons, 1790–1820*, 5 vols. (1986) · W. Cobbett and J. Wright, eds., *Cobbett's parliamentary history of England*, 36 vols. (1806–20), vol. 16, 1770; vol. 24, 1783 · *The works of John Adams, second president of the United States*, ed. C. F. Adams, 10 vols. (1850–56) · C. E. Vulliamy, *Royal George: a study of King George III* (1937) · C. Hibbert, *George III: a personal history* (1998) · P. D. G. Thomas, 'George III and the American Revolution', *History*, new ser., 70 (1985), 16–31 · P. D. G. Thomas, 'Thoughts on the British constitution by George III in 1760', *Historical Research*, 60 (1987), 361–3 · I. R. Christie, 'George III and the historians: thirty years on', *History*, new ser., 71 (1986), 205–21 · H. Butterfield, 'George III and the constitution', *History*, new ser., 43 (1958), 14–33 · J. H. Plumb, 'New light on the tyrant George III', *The American experience: the collected essays of J. H. Plumb* (1989), 50–60 · *Gentleman's Magazine*, 1st ser., 8 (1738), 323 · *Gentleman's Magazine*, 1st ser., 90/1 (1820), 172–6 · C. Lloyd, *The quest for Albion: monarchy and the patronage of British painting* (1998) · M. Levey, *The later Italian pictures in the collection of her majesty the queen* (1964) · O. Millar, *The later Georgian pictures in the collection of her majesty the queen*, 2 vols. (1969) · *A king's purchase: King George III and the collection of Consul Smith* (1994) · E. Miller, *That noble cabinet: a history of the British Museum* (1974) · J. Burke, *A general [*later edns *A genealogical] and heraldic dictionary of the peerage and baronetage of the United Kingdom [*later edns *the British empire]* (1829–)

Index

Enjoy biography? Explore more than 55,000 life stories in the Oxford Dictionary of National Biography

The biographies in the 'Very Interesting People' series derive from the *Oxford Dictionary of National Biography*—available in 60 print volumes and online.

To find out about the lives of more than 55,000 people who shaped all aspects of Britain's past worldwide, visit the *Oxford DNB* website at **www.oxforddnb.com**.

There's lots to discover ...

Read about remarkable people in all walks of life—not just the great and good, but those who left a mark, be they good, bad, or bizarre.

Browse through more than 10,000 portrait illustrations— the largest selection of national portraiture ever published.

Regular features on history in the news—with links to biographies—provide fascinating insights into topical events.

Get a life ... by email

Why not sign up to receive the free *Oxford DNB* 'Life of the Day' by email? Entertaining, informative, and topical biographies delivered direct to your inbox—a great way to start the day.

Find out more at www.oxforddnb.com

'An intellectual wonderland for all scholars and enthusiasts'

Tristram Hunt, *The Times*